GOOD FAST EATS

Delicious and Nutritious Family Meals Made Quickly

GOOD FAST EATS

From the Kitchen of **AMY FLANIGAN** at **bellyfull.net**

FRONT TABLE BOOKS | AN IMPRINT OF CEDAR FORT, INC. | SPRINGVILLE, UTAH

ISBN 13: 978-1-4621-1946-2

Published by Front Table Books, an imprint of Cedar Fort, Inc.
2373 W. 700 S., Springville, UT 84663
Distributed by Cedar Fort, Inc., www.cedarfort.com

LIBRARY OF CONGRESS CATALOGING-IN-PUBLICATION

Names: Flanigan, Amy, 1969- author.
Title: Good, fast eats / Amy Flanigan.
Description: Springville, Utah : Front Table Books, an imprint of Cedar Fort, Inc., [2016] | Includes index.
Identifiers: LCCN 2016027553 (print) | LCCN 2016029756 (ebook) | ISBN 9781462119462 (layflat binding : acid-free paper) | ISBN 9781462127214 (epub, pdf, mobi)
Subjects: LCSH: Quick and easy cooking. | LCGFT: Cookbooks.
Classification: LCC TX833.5 .F645 20016 (print) | LCC TX833.5 (ebook) | DDC 641.5/12--dc23
LC record available at https://lccn.loc.gov/2016027553

Cover and page design by M. Shaun McMurdie
Cover design © 2016 by Cedar Fort, Inc.
Edited by Jessica Romrell and Justin Greer

Printed in the United States of America

10 9 8 7 6 5 4 3 2 1

Printed on acid-free paper

To Paul – my absolute everything.

To Haley and Trevor – my loves. my life.

Contents

Introduction

I seem to have misplaced my sous chef. Oh, you too? I get it. I live in the real world with a job, husband, kids, a house, and no time to spend two hours making dinner. I don't even want to do that on the weekend! So I'm always on a mission to create delicious meals, using mostly fresh ingredients, that are easy and don't leave me fetal by the end of the day.

Long gone are the days when you got married, had a few kids, one spouse worked, while the other stayed home, kids played in the neighborhood and just had to be home by dinnertime. Maybe they had a dance class or football practice once a week.

Now, more and more couples depend on two incomes, play dates have to be scheduled, and sports activities are all week long, often overlapping with another commitment. Is it any wonder we're all exhausted?

Because of tight schedules and the constant juggling act, Fast Food has become commonplace. My kids are no strangers to it. Fast Food has definitely saved me on many occasions when I just couldn't bear the idea of washing one more bowl. But I believe it should be enjoyed in moderation. Just like everything.

My kitchen is proof that food can be fast and delicious, without self-loathing after eating it!

With a well-stocked spice drawer, pantry, and refrigerator, you can make magic happen often with only one bowl, one skillet, or one pot, all in just minutes.

So, to all the millions of parents who are struggling to put healthier meals on the table without breaking their back or the bank—I feel you!

Whenever talking to a friend or someone I just met, and hearing about how stressful dinnertime is for them, I cry a little inside. Meeting a massive deadline at work or trying to figure out how to pay for your kids' college is undeniably stressful, but dinnertime shouldn't be!

Here are some tips to get food on the table without tears or needing Xanax.

MENU PLAN

Waiting until the 11th hour to think about what you're going to make for dinner, as you and the family grow ravenous, is the kiss of death! I create my menu on Thursday, shop on Friday, and make the meals with fresh produce earlier in the week, so the food doesn't spoil. It's a routine that never fails me. Pick a schedule that works for you. Bookmark or print out recipes throughout the week that catch your eye, create your list, double check your pantry so you don't buy ingredients unnecessarily, then organize your list by item location in the grocery store, which will making shopping faster, too.

READ THROUGH EACH RECIPE BEFORE YOU START

There's nothing worse than getting halfway through making a recipe and realizing the pan needs to be covered, but the one you're using doesn't have a lid. Or you were supposed to save some of the pasta water, after you already drained it all. Or discovering that grilled steak you've been craving all day, needed to marinate overnight. Read through the entire recipe, and then read it again! This will ensure no surprises.

GATHER AND PREP ALL YOUR INGREDIENTS AND TOOLS BEFORE YOU START COOKING

You don't want to be sautéing that garlic, only to realize you never peeled the carrots that get added to the pan next - and then yikes! - the garlic burns. Or you need three cups of broth, but don't have your measuring cup, and then you can't find it! Unless otherwise noted in a recipe, you should always gather up all your ingredients and tools and prepare them before you start cooking, for smoother sailing.

PAY ATTENTION TO THE DETAILS

The difference between 1 teaspoon of coarse salt and 1 teaspoon of table salt can alter the taste of a recipe. The difference between 1/2-cup chopped parsley and a 1/2-cup parsley, chopped, and a chopped onion or a diced onion, matters. So, pay attention to the details.

ALWAYS FOLLOW A RECIPE EXACTLY HOW IT IS WRITTEN THE FIRST TIME YOU MAKE IT

I understand that you may have dietary restrictions or simply do not have a particular ingredient on hand, or are pressed for time. But by using substitutions or not following directions, it can (and probably will), change the overall outcome of a dish. Whether you're a novice or seasoned cook, I recommend you follow a recipe exactly how it's written the first time you make it. This will deliver optimal results. After that, if you have experience altering ingredients with a good outcome, then by all means, change things up to your personal preference!

Failures and mishaps can happen while cooking - I'm certainly not immune to that! But trial and error is an important part of how we learn in the kitchen! Relax and have fun with it.

Stock Up!

I used to enjoy grocery shopping; going up and down every aisle, seeing what new products were available, and smelling all the gourmet cheeses.

Then I had kids.

Going to the market became such a headache—all you parents of young ones know what I'm talking about! Now they're older, so it's not such a hassle. But the pleasure that once was might never return. It's just another chore, like getting gasoline or emptying the dishwasher.

I combat the dreaded task by stocking up on as many non-perishable goods as possible, decreasing the number of trips per week. But also, keeping a well-stocked and organized spice drawer, pantry, and refrigerator helps make meal planning easier!

While this list is not all-inclusive, it has the essentials that I have on hand at all times and will allow you to make the recipes in this book. They are all versatile but commonly used foods available at any market.

SPICE DRAWER

Table salt	Onion powder
Kosher salt	Garlic powder
Sea salt	Chili powder
Ground black pepper	Curry powder
Black peppercorns	Cayenne pepper
Cracked red pepper flakes	Paprika
Cumin	Old Bay
Italian blend	Bay leaves
Oregano	Cinnamon
Thyme	Baking powder
Cajun spice blend	Baking soda
Coriander	Vanilla extract
Ground ginger	

Pasta of all different shapes and sizes

Broth - chicken, beef, and vegetable (cans and cartons)

Grains - white rice, brown rice, quinoa, couscous

Nuts - almonds, walnuts, pecans, pine nuts

Dried fruit - dark and golden raisins, cranberries, cherries, apricots

Oatmeal - regular, instant, and steel cut

Cornmeal

Breadcrumbs

Canned beans - black, pinto, kidney, navy, garbanzo

Canned corn

Flour

Granulated sugar

Brown sugar

Cornstarch

Honey

An assortment of jams and jellies

Semi-sweet chocolate chips

White chocolate chips

Nonstick spray

Good quality white wine (such as Chardonnay, Pinot, or Sauvignon Blanc)

Sauces - Hoisin Sauce, Chili Garlic Sauce, Low Sodium Soy Sauce, Worcestershire sauce, Sriracha hot sauce, salsa

Oils - Sesame oil, Extra Virgin Olive Oil, Canola oil, Vegetable Oil

Vinegars - Rice wine vinegar, Apple cider vinegar, Balsamic vinegar, red and white wine vinegar

REFRIGERATOR	MUST HAVE PRODUCE
Milk	Potatoes
Orange Juice	Carrots
Eggs	Onions
Unsalted butter	Garlic
Sour Cream	Ginger
Greek Yogurt	Lemons
An assorted of cheeses	Limes
Ginger paste	Scallions
Bacon	Parsley
Mayonnaise	
Ketchup	
Mustard	

If you have the ability, I highly recommend growing your own herbs. Sometimes fresh is better utilized than dried in certain recipes, and you can save a bundle of money by just trimming off a few sprigs, as opposed to buying a bulk that you don't need.

CHICKEN

Easy Cashew Chicken

Chicken Tenderloins with Creamy Mustard
and Thyme Sauce

Honey-Sesame Chicken Salad Wraps

Sweet and Sour Chicken

Sautéed Chicken with Olive Orzo

Sweet and Spicy Chicken Black Bean Enchiladas

Szechuan Chicken and Snap Peas

Easy Cashew Chicken

Forget the takeout and cook in with this super easy Chinese-American dish, where chicken and cashews are tossed in a sweet Hoisin sauce. It's simple, flavorful, and also great the next day if you have any left over, making it one of my favorite weekday dinners.

SERVES: 4 **PREP TIME:** 15 Minutes **COOK TIME:** 15 Minutes **TOTAL TIME:** 30 Minutes

INGREDIENTS:

- 3 Tbsp. hoisin sauce
- ½ tsp. chili garlic sauce
- 3 Tbsp. water
- 1½ lb. boneless, skinless chicken thighs, cut into 1-inch pieces
- salt and pepper
- 1 Tbsp. cornstarch

- 1½ Tbsp. vegetable oil
- 1 small sweet onion, cut into 1-inch pieces
- 4 garlic cloves, minced
- 2 Tbsp. rice vinegar
- 6 scallions, diced
- ¾ cup unsalted, roasted cashews
- cooked white rice

DIRECTIONS:

In a small bowl, whisk together the hoisin sauce, chili garlic sauce, and water. Set aside.

In a medium bowl, season the chicken with a few grinds of salt and pepper and toss with the cornstarch until coated.

In a large nonstick pan, heat the oil over medium-high heat. Sauté the chicken, tossing often, until browned and cooked, about 10 minutes. Add the onion and cook for 3 minutes until soft and translucent, stirring frequently. Add garlic and cook for 15 seconds until fragrant. Add the rice vinegar and deglaze the pan, scraping up any brown bits, about 1 minute.

Reduce heat to medium-low. Add the hoisin mixture; cook, tossing to combine and warm through, about 1 more minute.

Remove from heat and stir in the scallions and cashews. Season with a little more salt and pepper if necessary.

Serve over cooked hot white rice.

Chicken Tenderloins with Creamy Mustard and Thyme Sauce

This incredibly simple mustard sauce elevates ho-hum chicken within minutes. It's creamy and luscious, tangy and rich. Sometimes I just make it to drizzle over roasted vegetables.

SERVES: 4 **PREP TIME:** 15 Minutes **COOK TIME:** 15 Minutes **TOTAL TIME:** 30 Minutes

INGREDIENTS:

- 1½ lb. chicken breast tenderloins
- salt and pepper
- ¼ cup flour
- 2-3 Tbsp. extra virgin olive oil
- 1 large shallot, diced

- 1 cup low-sodium chicken broth
- 2 sprigs of fresh thyme
- ¼ cup heavy whipping cream
- 1 Tbsp. spicy brown mustard

DIRECTIONS:

Sprinkle the chicken tenderloins on both sides with salt and pepper. Dredge in the flour and shake off any excess.

Heat 2 tablespoons oil in a large skillet over medium-high heat. Add chicken; cook for 4 minutes on each side (adding the additional tablespoon of oil once you turn them, only if needed). Transfer to a plate and keep warm.

Add shallots to the pan; sauté 1-2 minutes until softened. Stir in the broth and thyme sprigs; bring liquid to a boil and simmer for a couple of minutes. Stir in the whipping cream and simmer for 1-2 minutes more to thicken. Stir in the mustard. Remove from heat and discard the thyme. Serve chicken immediately with pan sauce.

NOTES: *Serve with grilled asparagus, roasted broccoli, or a side salad.*

Honey-Sesame Chicken Salad Wraps

I think salad is a tough one to get kids on board with. But both of mine actually like it, and I'm as happy about that as one can imagine! One of their favorites is an Asian Chicken Salad with Honey-Sesame dressing that I make for dinner quite often. I adapted it for wraps, so they could easily enjoy it at school, too.

SERVES: 4 **PREP TIME:** 15 Minutes **COOK TIME:** 20 Minutes **TOTAL TIME:** 35 Minutes

INGREDIENTS:

For the dressing

- ⅓ cup honey
- ½ cup mayonnaise
- 2 tsp. Dijon mustard
- 3 Tbsp. rice wine vinegar
- 1 tsp. sesame oil

For the wraps

- 4 large pieces Tyson's Crispy Chicken Strips
- 4 (10-inch) burrito sized flour tortillas
- 2 cups broccoli slaw, divided
- ¼ cup sliced almonds, divided

DIRECTIONS:

In a small bowl, whisk together the honey, mayonnaise, mustard, vinegar, and sesame oil. Refrigerate until ready to make the wraps.

Bake the chicken strips according to the package directions (about 20 minutes.) Remove and allow to cool slightly. Slice up, crosswise, into thin pieces.

Spread 1½ tablespoons of the dressing on the tortilla, leaving a 1-inch border. Sprinkle ½ cup of the broccoli slaw down the middle, followed by 1 tablespoon of the almonds, and the chicken pieces on top. Drizzle another 1½ tablespoons of dressing over the top of the chicken. Roll up like a burrito. Repeat with the remaining ingredients.

Eat whole or cut in half.

Sweet and Sour Chicken

This homemade Sweet and Sour Chicken rivals any restaurant version. And in about the time it takes to have it delivered, you could already be eating!

SERVES: 6 **PREP TIME:** 15 Minutes **COOK TIME:** 15 Minutes **TOTAL TIME:** 30 Minutes

INGREDIENTS:

- 1½ Tbsp. cornstarch, divided
- 1 Tbsp. water
- ⅓ cup rice wine vinegar
- ⅓ cup brown sugar
- 3 Tbsp. ketchup
- 1½ Tbsp. low-sodium soy sauce
- 1 can (8-oz.) pineapple chunks, drained, juice reserved
- 2 Tbsp. vegetable oil

- 1½ lb. boneless, skinless chicken breasts, cut into bite-sized pieces
- salt and pepper
- 1 small red bell pepper, cut into 1-inch pieces
- 1 small green bell pepper, cut into 1-inch pieces
- 1 small sweet onion, cut into 1-inch pieces
- cooked white rice

DIRECTIONS:

In a medium bowl, whisk together 1 tablespoon of the cornstarch and water, until combined. Whisk in the rice wine vinegar, brown sugar, ketchup, soy sauce, and reserved pineapple juice. Set aside.

In a large nonstick skillet, warm the vegetable oil over medium-high. Toss the chicken with the remaining ½ tablespoon cornstarch, and season with salt and pepper. Add to the skillet and cook, without stirring for 2–3 minutes. Mix and continue to sauté for another 6–7 minutes. With a slotted spoon, transfer chicken to a plate.

Add red bell pepper, green bell pepper, and onion to the skillet; cook for 3 minutes until vegetables soften and get a bit charred. Season with salt and pepper. Pour in the sweet and sour sauce mixture, along with the pineapple chunks. Cook for another 1–2 minutes to warm through and allow sauce to thicken slightly. Add chicken back to skillet and stir to combine.

Serve over cooked white rice and enjoy!

Sautéed Chicken with Olive Orzo

Chicken recipes are plenty, but I always struggle with side dishes to go with them. Orzo pasta is like a blank canvas that can easily be dressed up, in this case with olives, Parmesan, and parsley, and pairs wonderfully with pan-seared chicken. This meal is healthy and flavorful, comforting and simple.

SERVES: 4 **PREP TIME:** 15 Minutes **COOK TIME:** 10 Minutes **TOTAL TIME:** 25 Minutes

INGREDIENTS:

For the orzo

- 1 can (15-oz.) low-sodium chicken broth
- ¾ cup uncooked orzo pasta
- 1 can (2.25-oz.) sliced black olives, drained
- ¼ cup grated Parmesan cheese
- ¼ cup chopped parsley
- 1 Tbsp. extra virgin olive oil
- freshly ground black pepper

For the chicken

- ½ Tbsp. dried oregano
- ¼ tsp. salt
- ¼ tsp. pepper
- 4 boneless, skinless chicken breast halves (about 4 ounces each, flattened to ¼-inch thickness)
- ⅓ cup flour
- 1 Tbsp. extra virgin olive oil
- 2 Tbsp. unsalted butter
- 2 Tbsp. chicken broth
- 1 Tbsp lemon juice

DIRECTIONS:

Bring chicken stock to a boil in a medium pot. Add orzo, reduce heat to a strong simmer, and cook until pasta is tender and liquid is absorbed, stirring several times to prevent sticking, about 10 minutes. Mix in the olives, Parmesan, parsley, olive oil, and a couple grinds of black pepper.

While the Orzo is cooking, combine the oregano, salt, and pepper. Sprinkle over the chicken. Dredge chicken in the flour, shaking off any excess.

Heat oil and butter in a large nonstick skillet over medium-high. Cook chicken for 4 minutes per side; transfer to a plate and keep warm.

Add chicken broth and lemon juice to the pan, stirring a few times, scraping to loosen up any browned bits.

Place a chicken breast on each of 4 serving plates; spoon sauce over each breast and serve with the orzo.

Sweet and Spicy Chicken Black Bean Enchiladas

Enchiladas are one of my favorite things to make with leftover Thanksgiving turkey and cranberry sauce. They work equally great with rotisserie chicken. Mexican spices, black beans, and Monterey Jack cheese are added, creating an amazing circus of flavors!

MAKES: 16 **PREP TIME:** 20 Minutes **COOK TIME:** 20 Minutes **TOTAL TIME:** 40 Minutes

INGREDIENTS:

- 1 can (14-oz.) whole-berry cranberry sauce
- 1 can (10-oz.) enchilada sauce
- 2½ cups shredded rotisserie chicken, skin discarded
- ¾ cup canned black beans, rinsed and drained
- 3 scallions, chopped
- ¼ cup chopped fresh parsley

- ½ tsp. cumin
- ¼ tsp. garlic powder
- ¼ tsp. salt
- ¼ tsp. black pepper
- 2 cups shredded Monterey Jack Cheese, divided
- 16 (5-inch) good quality corn tortillas
- sour cream, for serving

DIRECTIONS:

Preheat oven to 350°F. Lightly coat a 9 x 13 casserole dish with nonstick cooking spray.

In a medium bowl, combine the cranberry sauce and enchilada sauce. Pour ½ cup of the sauce mixture in the bottom of the casserole dish.

In a large bowl, combine the chicken, beans, scallions, parsley, cumin, garlic powder, salt, pepper, 1 cup of the cheese, and another ½ cup of the cranberry sauce mixture.

Wrap tortillas in a dishtowel and warm in the microwave to make pliable.

Place ¼ cup of the filling on each tortilla; roll up and place seam-side down in the casserole dish. Cover with the remaining cranberry sauce and 1 cup of cheese.

Cover with foil; bake for 20 minutes until the cheese is melted and bubbly.

Serve with a sprinkle of chopped parsley and a dollop of sour cream.

NOTES: *If you have a favorite homemade enchilada sauce, feel free to use that instead.*

Szechuan Chicken and Snap Peas

My pantry is always stocked with Asian flavor staples; they can transform just about any pasta or rice dish, and are a great way to elevate plain ground meat. This quick and easy stir-fry with snap peas and chicken has the perfect amount of zing. If you're lucky enough to have anything leftover, this also makes a good lunch the next day!

SERVES: 4 **PREP TIME:** 15 Minutes **COOK TIME:** 10 Minutes **TOTAL TIME:** 25 Minutes

INGREDIENTS:

- 3 Tbsp. low-sodium soy sauce
- ½ Tbsp. sesame oil
- 1 Tbsp. hoisin sauce
- 1 Tbsp. honey
- 2 tsp. chili garlic sauce
- 1 Tbsp. vegetable oil
- 1 lb. ground chicken
- salt and pepper

- 6 oz. snap peas
- 1 medium sweet onion, cut into 1-inch pieces
- 3 garlic cloves, minced
- 2 Tbsp. minced fresh ginger
- 2 Tbsp. rice wine vinegar
- 1 can (8-oz.) sliced water chestnuts, drained
- cooked white rice, for serving

DIRECTIONS:

In a medium bowl, whisk together the soy sauce, sesame oil, hoisin, honey, and chili garlic sauce. Set aside.

Heat oil in a large nonstick skillet or wok over medium-high. Add ground chicken; cook until browned and no pink remains, breaking it up with a wooden spoon as it cooks, about 3 minutes. Season with salt and pepper. Drain off fat.

Add in snap peas, onion, garlic, and ginger. Sauté for 3 minutes. Pour in the rice wine; when it is mostly evaporated, give the soy sauce mixture a whirl and add it to the skillet, along with the water chestnuts. Sauté for another 3–4 more minutes. Taste and adjust seasoning, if necessary.

Serve over cooked white rice.

PORK

Asian Pork Tenderloin with
Raisin-Almond Couscous

Teriyaki Pork Stir Fry

Kielbasa and Cabbage Skillet

Sausage and Pea Pasta

Moo Shu Pork

Creamy Spaghettini with Sausage and Spinach

Italian Sausage and Peppers Skillet

Pan-Seared Pork Chops with Onions,
Raisins, and Baby Peas

Asian Pork Tenderloin with Raisin-Almond Couscous

I just adore recipes that look elegant, but are so easy to make. This is one of them! Dried fruit pairs with pork just as well as fresh fruit. This next recipe, which uses raisins, is the perfect example of the combination of pork and fruit to create a flavor-saturated, delicious dish. I like regular raisins for added color, but golden raisins work great, too.

SERVES: 4 **PREP TIME:** 10 minutes + marinate overnight **COOK TIME:** 20 Minutes
TOTAL TIME: 30 minutes, not including marinating

INGREDIENTS:

For the pork marinade
- 1 (1¼ lb.) pork tenderloin
- 2 Tbsp. low-sodium soy sauce
- 2 Tbsp. hoisin sauce
- 1 Tbsp. rice wine vinegar
- 1 Tbsp. black bean sauce
- 1 tsp. minced fresh ginger
- 1 large clove garlic, minced
- 2 tsp. brown sugar
- 1 tsp. sesame oil
- ⅛ tsp. allspice

For the couscous
- 3 Tbsp. vegetable oil, divided
- ½ cup raisins
- 1½ cups low-sodium chicken broth + a splash
- 1 cup couscous
- ⅓ cup sliced almonds
- 3 scallions, diced
- 2 Tbsp. lemon juice
- pinch of salt

DIRECTIONS:

Place pork in a large resealable plastic bag. In a medium bowl, whisk together all the marinade ingredients; pour over the pork, making sure it gets coated all over. Seal the bag, pressing out any excess air. Refrigerate overnight.

Preheat oven to 425°F.

Heat a large ovenproof skillet over medium-high. Add 1 tablespoon of the oil; swirl to coat. Discard pork marinade and add the tenderloin to the pan; sear 4 minutes. Turn pork over; place pan in oven for 15 minutes or until a thermometer registers 145°F. Remove skillet from oven (careful, handle will be hot!) and transfer pork to a cutting board. Let stand 10 minutes.

While the pork rests, place raisins in a small bowl filled with hot water. Let stand for 10 minutes to plump up; drain.

Simultaneously, make the couscous. In a medium pot, bring the 1½ cups chicken broth to a boil; add couscous, cover, and remove from the heat. Let stand 5 minutes. Uncover, fluff with a fork, and gently toss in the remaining 2 tablespoons oil, raisins, almonds, scallions, lemon juice, and a pinch of salt.

Add a splash of chicken broth to the skillet to loosen up any brown bits. Cut the pork into thin slices; divide onto plates and serve with the couscous. Drizzle some of the pan juices over the top. Serve immediately.

Teriyaki Pork Stir Fry

*Anything with **Hawaiian** or **Teriyaki** in the title of a recipe immediately gets my attention. I just love the flavors associated with both. I make this stir-fry all the time; it's so tasty and a lifesaver on busy weeknights, on the table in only 20 minutes!*

SERVES: 4-6 **PREP TIME:** 10 Minutes **COOK TIME:** 10 Minutes **TOTAL TIME:** 20 Minutes

INGREDIENTS:

- 1 Tbsp. sesame oil, divided
- 6 oz. broccoli slaw
- salt and pepper
- 1½ lb. ground pork
- 2 garlic cloves, minced
- 1 tsp. ginger paste
- 1 tsp. chili garlic sauce
- ½ cup good quality teriyaki sauce
- 3 scallions, cut into 1-inch pieces
- juice from one large lime
- cooked white rice

DIRECTIONS:

In a large nonstick skillet, warm half of the sesame oil over medium-high heat. Add broccoli slaw to the hot pan and sauté for about 2-3 minutes until almost tender. Season with salt and pepper to taste; transfer to a bowl.

Add the remaining sesame oil to the skillet, followed by the pork, garlic, ginger, and chili garlic sauce. Cook pork, stirring often, breaking it up with a wooden spoon until no pink remains, about 3-4 minutes. Season with salt and pepper. Drain off fat.

Stir in the teriyaki sauce. Add slaw back in, along with the scallions and lime juice; mix to coat.

Serve over hot cooked white rice.

NOTES: *Use a good quality thick teriyaki sauce for this, not a thin marinade.*

Kielbasa and Cabbage Skillet

Paul's not a fan of cabbage, but he seems to love it in this dish—probably because it soaks up a lot of the rendered fat from the pork. This one-pan skillet dinner has been in my Top 5 recipes on Belly Full since I originally shared it in 2014, garnering hundreds of positive reviews. It's great for any weeknight when you need something easy and fast. I altered it slightly by adding in some roasted potatoes, which took it up another level. Make it and see what all the fuss is about!

SERVES: 4 **PREP TIME:** 15 Minutes **COOK TIME:** 20 Minutes **TOTAL TIME:** 35 Minutes

INGREDIENTS:

- ½ pound small new potatoes, quartered
- 1½ Tbsp. extra virgin olive oil, divided
- salt and pepper
- 1 log (14-oz.) fully cooked polska kielbasa, cut in half lengthwise, then cut into 2-inch pieces
- 1 small head cabbage, core removed, coarsely chopped (about 6 cups)
- 1 large sweet onion, cut into large pieces

- 3 cloves garlic, minced
- 2 tsp. granulated sugar
- ½ tsp. salt
- ½ tsp. black pepper
- 2 tsp. rice wine vinegar
- 1½ tsp. Dijon or brown grainy mustard

DIRECTIONS:

Preheat oven to 400°F. Place potatoes on a baking sheet. Drizzle with ½ tablespoon olive oil and sprinkle with some salt and pepper; toss to coat. Cook for 18-20 minutes until tender, but not mushy.

Heat the remaining tablespoon of olive oil in a large nonstick sauté pan over medium-high and add kielbasa. Cook without stirring for 1 minute. Then stir occasionally for about 3 minutes. Transfer to a plate with a slotted spoon.

In the same pan with some of the rendered kielbasa fat, add the cabbage, onion, garlic, sugar, salt, and pepper. Stir to combine and cook for 8-10 minutes. Mix in the vinegar and mustard; add the sausage back to the pan and cook for another 2 minutes, to heat through. Toss in the roasted potatoes. Taste and adjust seasoning, if necessary.

Serve immediately and enjoy!

Sausage and Pea Pasta

My daughter has always been good about eating vegetables. Her younger brother? Not so much. But he loves this pasta dish, so I make it often. It's quick and flavorful, where ground pork sausage and baby peas shine, and at least in my house, the peas don't get picked out!

SERVES: 6 **PREP TIME:** 10 Minutes **COOK TIME:** 15 Minutes **TOTAL TIME:** 25 Minutes

INGREDIENTS:

- 1 lb. rotini pasta
- 2 Tbsp. extra virgin olive oil
- 1 small sweet onion, finely diced
- 2 garlic cloves, minced
- 1 lb. sweet Italian sausage links, casings removed
- salt and freshly ground pepper

- ⅛ tsp. crushed red pepper flakes
- ½ tsp dried oregano
- 1 can (15-oz.) diced tomatoes, undrained
- ½ cup low-sodium chicken broth
- ¾ cup frozen sweet peas, thawed
- ¼ cup half-n-half
- Parmesan for serving, optional

DIRECTIONS:

Bring a large pot of salted water to boil. Cook the pasta to al dente texture, according to package instructions.

In the meantime, heat the olive oil in a large nonstick skillet over medium-high heat. Add the onion, garlic, and sausage; sauté, breaking up the pork into small pieces with a wooden spoon, until no pink remains and the onions are softened, about 4 minutes. Drain off fat. Season with a couple grinds of salt and pepper, the crushed red pepper flakes, and oregano.

Add in the tomatoes with their liquid, and chicken broth. Turn heat down to medium and gently simmer for 5–10 minutes, until the pasta is done cooking. Toss in the peas along with the half-and-half; mix and warm through.

Drain the pasta and return to the pot. Stir in the sausage mixture until thoroughly combined. Ladle into bowls and serve right away with a sprinkle of Parmesan, if desired.

Moo Shu Pork

Growing up, there used to be this great little Chinese restaurant near our house. Every couple of months my Dad would call in a big order, and it always included Moo Shu Pork. I think it was my mom's favorite.

It's a savory stir-fry dish made with pork, Napa cabbage, and shiitake mushrooms, which are rolled up in Mandarin pancakes, painted with sweet hoisin sauce.

I've simplified the dish by using flour tortillas, instead of the traditional wrapper. Don't be overwhelmed by the long list of ingredients; most of it requires very little preparation, and the entire dish comes together in just 30 minutes.

SERVES: 4 **PREP TIME:** 20 Minutes **COOK TIME:** 8 Minutes **TOTAL TIME:** 30 Minutes

INGREDIENTS:

- 2 Tbsp. low-sodium soy sauce
- 2 Tbsp. rice wine vinegar
- 1 tsp. sesame oil
- 1½ tsp. cornstarch
- 1 lb. pork loin, cut into long, thin strips
- 4 Tbsp. vegetable oil, divided
- 3 eggs, lightly beaten
- 3 garlic cloves, minced

- 1 Tbsp. minced fresh ginger
- 2 cups coleslaw mix
- 1½ cups bean sprouts
- 8 oz. shiitake mushrooms, sliced
- 8 scallions stalks, trimmed, cut into 2-inch pieces
- coarse salt and freshly ground black pepper
- ½ cup hoisin sauce, divided
- 8 (8-inch) flour tortillas

DIRECTIONS:

In large bowl, whisk together the soy sauce, rice wine vinegar, sesame oil, and cornstarch until combined. Toss in the pork, making sure all the pieces are coated. Set aside while you prep the other ingredients.

Heat 1 tablespoon of the oil in a wok over high heat. Add eggs and swirl to coat the surface of the wok. Cook, without stirring, until set, 1 to 2 minutes. Transfer to a cutting board; roll up and slice crosswise into ¼-inch wide strips; set aside. Wipe wok clean.

Heat the remaining 3 tablespoons of the oil in a wok over high heat. Add the pork, stir quickly for 1 minute; transfer to a bowl with a slotted spoon.

With remaining oil in wok, add in the garlic and ginger; stir for a few seconds. Toss in the coleslaw, sprouts, mushrooms, and scallions. Cook, stirring, for 2–3 minutes until vegetables are soft. Season with a pinch of salt and pepper.

Add the pork back to the wok, along with ⅓ cup of hoisin sauce. Mix to combine. Taste, and add a pinch more salt and pepper, if necessary. Transfer filling to a bowl.

Stack tortillas between damp paper towels; microwave on high for 1–2 minutes. Lay individual tortillas on plates, paint the remaining hoisin on each one; top with the moo shu filling and the egg strips. Roll up and enjoy!

Creamy Spaghettini with Sausage and Spinach

This was one of the first recipes I developed for the book, inspired by my Sausage and Tortellini soup, which is a family favorite. And it was everything I hoped it would be. Creamy, rich, hearty, and all made in one pot!

SERVES: 6 **PREP TIME:** 10 Minutes **COOK TIME:** 25 Minutes **TOTAL TIME:** 35 Minutes

INGREDIENTS:

- 3 tsp. extra virgin olive oil
- 1 lb. sweet Italian sausage links
- 1 medium sweet onion, diced
- 3 garlic cloves, minced
- salt and freshly ground black pepper

- 32 oz. low-sodium chicken broth
- ¼ cup water
- 12 oz. thin spaghetti, broken in half
- 5 oz. fresh baby spinach
- ⅓ cup heavy whipping cream

DIRECTIONS:

Heat oil over medium in a Dutch oven. Add sausages and cook, rolling occasionally, until browned all over, about 10 minutes. Transfer to a paper towel-lined plate and pour off all but 1 tablespoon fat from the pot.

Add onion to the pot and cook until softened, about 3 minutes, scraping up any browned bits. Add garlic and cook for about 30 seconds. Season with a touch of salt and pepper. Pour in broth and water; turn heat up to high and bring to a boil.

Stir in the pasta and simmer until tender, about 7 minutes.

In the meantime, slice sausage in half lengthwise and then into bite size pieces. Add back to the pot with the pasta and cook for another 1–2 minutes.

Stir in spinach and cook until just wilted. Add cream; warm through.

Serve immediately in individual bowls with a little grind of black pepper.

NOTES: *This recipe calls for **thin** spaghetti, which is in between regular and angel hair. Make sure that's what you use, or the cooking time and amount of broth will need to be adjusted.*

Italian Sausage and Peppers Skillet

Italian sausage links mingle with sweet bell peppers and onion in this simple skillet dish. Serve on hoagie rolls, or over polenta or mashed potatoes!

SERVES: 5 **PREP TIME:** 10 Minutes **COOK TIME:** 20 Minutes **TOTAL TIME:** 30 Minutes

INGREDIENTS:

- 1½ Tbsp extra virgin olive oil
- 5 sweet Italian sausage links, pricked a few times with a fork
- 3 small bell peppers, any color, sliced into thin strips
- 1 small red onion, sliced thin
- salt and pepper

- 3 garlic cloves, minced
- ⅛ tsp. cracked red pepper flakes
- 1 tsp. dried Italian seasoning
- ¼ cup low-sodium chicken broth
- ¾ cup golden raisins
- Toasted hoagie rolls, split

DIRECTIONS:

Heat oil over medium in a large nonstick skillet. Add sausages and cook, rolling occasionally, until browned all over, about 5 minutes. Transfer to a paper towel-lined plate; set aside.

Increase heat to medium-high, add bell peppers and onion to the pan and cook until softened, about 5 minutes, stirring often and scraping up any browned bits. Season with salt and pepper to taste. Add in the garlic, cracked red pepper, and Italian seasoning; stir to combine.

Pour in the chicken broth and add sausages back to the pan, along with the raisins; reduce heat to low. Cover and simmer until sausages are cooked through and no pink remains on the inside, about 10 minutes.

Serve on toasted hoagie rolls with some of the juices from the pan.

Pan-Seared Pork Chops with Onions, Raisins, and Baby Peas

My son is currently eight years old, and still refers to pork as chicken. I'm hoping to break him of this before he's an adult. Either way, pork is his favorite protein. Granted, he still requires mayonnaise along side a good chop, like these. But I'm not going to fight it, as long as he eats the vegetables too. I'll pick my battles!

This is such a simple and delicious weeknight meal that only takes 25 minutes. The intense seasoning on the pork balances perfectly with the sweetness of onions, raisins, and baby peas.

SERVES: 4 **PREP TIME:** 10 Minutes **COOK TIME:** 15 Minutes **TOTAL TIME:** 25 Minutes

INGREDIENTS:

- 2½ Tbsp. extra virgin olive oil, divided
- 2 medium onions, tip and root trimmed, cut in half, skins removed, sliced into half moons
- ½ cup low-sodium chicken broth
- ½ cup raisins
- ½ cup frozen sweet baby peas, defrosted
- 2 tsp. kosher salt
- ½ tsp. black pepper
- ½ tsp. ground coriander
- 2 thick-cut boneless pork chops (about 1¼ lb. total)

DIRECTIONS:

In a large skillet, heat 1 tablespoon of the oil over medium-high. Add the onions and mix to coat. Pour in the chicken broth; reduce heat to medium-low, cover, and cook for 10 minutes. Remove lid, toss in the raisins and peas and continue cooking for 5 minutes, stirring occasionally.

In the meantime, combine the salt, pepper, and coriander; rub seasoning mixture on both sides of the pork chops.

Heat another large skillet on high. Once it is very hot, add the remaining olive oil and then reduce the heat to medium. Add pork to the pan. Sear for 4-5 minutes on each side, until an internal temperature reaches 135°F. Transfer to a cutting board and allow to rest for 5 minutes, or until the internal temperature reaches 145°F.

Slice pork and serve with the onion mixture.

NOTES: *For pork chops, it's best to get the pan extremely hot, and then bring it down to medium. That first contact with the heat helps obtain that gorgeous golden crust, but if you keep it at high, the chops won't cook evenly through the middle. Turning down the heat to medium, helps keep the exterior tender, while the center reaches the ideal temperature.*

BEEF

Easy Ground Beef Stroganoff

Greek Meatball Pockets with Tzatziki

Vegetable Beef Stir-Fry

Slow Cooker Hoisin Pot Roast with Vegetables

Unstuffed Cabbage Roll Skillet

Beef and Potato Picadillo

Italian Meatball Skillet

Cumin-Lime Grilled Sirloin with
Roasted Vegetables

Easy Ground Beef Stroganoff

Beef stroganoff was one of my favorite meals growing up, but my mom used to use strips of sirloin. Here, it gets a little makeover with ground beef, lowering the cost and prep time, and it's just as delicious!

SERVES: 4-6 **PREP TIME:** 15 Minutes **COOK TIME:** 15 Minutes **TOTAL TIME:** 30 Minutes

INGREDIENTS:

- 12 oz. wide egg-free noodles
- 2 Tbsp. unsalted butter
- 1 medium sweet onion, finely diced
- 3 cloves garlic, minced
- 1 lb. lean ground beef
- 2 Tbsp. flour
- 2 tsp. coarse salt

- ¾ tsp. dried Italian herbs
- 1 can (6-oz.) tomato paste
- 1 can (10-oz.) condensed beef consommé
- 1 Tbsp. white wine vinegar
- 8 oz. sliced button or crimini mushrooms
- 1 cup sour cream

DIRECTIONS:

Bring a large pot of water to boil. Cook noodles according to package directions, al dente.

In a large nonstick skillet, heat the butter over medium-high. Add onion and garlic. Sauté until softened, about 3 minutes. Add ground beef and brown, breaking it up with a wooden spoon until no pink remains, 3-4 minutes. Drain off fat.

Mix in the flour, salt, and herbs. Stir in tomato paste, consommé, vinegar, and mushrooms. Turn down heat to medium and simmer, uncovered, stirring occasionally for 10 minutes or until mushrooms are tender.

Remove from heat and stir in the sour cream until combined and heated through.

Serve sauce on top of the cooked noodles.

Greek Meatball Pockets with Tzatziki

If meatballs and gyros had a shotgun wedding, this is what their baby might look like! Meatballs cooked in Greek seasoning, with a cool yogurt-cucumber sauce to balance out all the flavors perfectly, served in a pita pocket. No utensils needed!

SERVES: 4 **PREP TIME:** 15 Minutes **COOK TIME:** 10 Minutes **TOTAL TIME:** 25 Minutes

INGREDIENTS:

- 16 homemade or store-bought plain meatballs, thawed if frozen
- 2 tsp. Greek seasoning
- 2 whole perforated pita pockets, split in half
- ¾ cup plain Greek yogurt

- ¼ cup diced cucumber
- 3 Tbsp. finely diced red onion, divided
- 1 tsp. finely diced fresh mint
- ¼ tsp. kosher salt
- ⅓ cup sliced and halved cucumber

DIRECTIONS:

Toss the meatballs with the Greek seasoning and place on a baking sheet in a single layer. Bake according to package directions when thawed. When you have 5 minutes remaining, place your flatbreads on another baking sheet and warm in the oven.

In the meantime, make your sauce. Whisk together the yogurt, diced cucumber, 1 tablespoon onion, mint, and salt.

Spread some sauce in each pita half, followed by a few cucumber slices. Stuff with 3-4 meatballs, depending on their size.

Serve immediately and enjoy!

NOTES: *Since you'll be seasoning the meatballs with Greek spices, make sure you purchase plain ones, not Italian flavored. Or feel free to make your own!*

Vegetable Beef Stir-Fry

I could eat stir-fry every single day and never get tired of it. By changing up the type of protein and/or vegetables, you can have a different dish every time. And it's so easy! This recipe calls for thin strips of sirloin, beautifully colored green beans and red bell pepper, cooked in a classic Asian sauce.

SERVES: 6 **PREP TIME:** 20 Minutes **COOK TIME:** 10 Minutes **TOTAL TIME:** 30 Minutes

INGREDIENTS:

- ½ cup low-sodium soy sauce
- 3 Tbsp. rice wine vinegar
- 2 Tbsp. brown sugar
- 2 Tbsp. cornstarch
- 1 Tbsp. minced fresh ginger
- 1½ lb. beef sirloin, fat trimmed and sliced very thin
- 2 Tbsp. vegetable oil, divided
- 1 small sweet onion, diced

- 6 oz. green beans, trimmed, cut into 1-inch pieces
- 1 small red bell pepper, core removed, cut into 1-inch strips
- 2 garlic cloves, minced
- salt and pepper
- ¼ tsp. red pepper flakes
- 3 scallions, diced
- cooked white rice

DIRECTIONS:

In a bowl, mix together soy sauce, rice vinegar, brown sugar, cornstarch, and ginger. Add sliced meat to bowl and toss with hands. Set aside.

In a large nonstick skillet, heat 1 tablespoon of the vegetable oil over medium-high. Add the onion, green beans, and bell pepper to the hot pan and sauté, stirring every 45 seconds, for about 6–7 minutes until tender and charred. Add in the garlic and cook for 15 seconds until fragrant. Season with salt and pepper to taste; transfer to a bowl.

Add ½ tablespoon of oil to pan and allow to get very hot again. With tongs, add half the meat by spreading it out in the skillet, leaving most of the marinade still in the bowl. Let the meat sear without stirring for one minute. Turn meat over and cook for another 30 seconds. Transfer to a clean plate.

Repeat with other half of meat. After turning it, add the first plateful of meat, the rest of the marinade from the bowl, the vegetables, red pepper flakes, and scallions. Stir over high heat for 30 seconds and then turn off heat. Check seasonings and add a touch of salt, only if necessary. Mixture will thicken as it sits.

Serve immediately over cooked white rice.

Slow Cooker Hoisin Pot Roast with Vegetables

Long time readers of Belly Full know I sort of have a love-hate relationship with slow cooker recipes. I find most of them to be disappointing; either bland, or made up of too many cream-of-soup canned goods, rendering a big bowl of mush at the end of 8 hours. But, oh how I adore the ones that turn out, because there's nothing like coming home at the end of the day, knowing dinner is already taken care of!

THIS is one of those success stories. Chuck roast cooks in a sweet and sour liquid bath all day, delivering meat that shreds like butter, alongside tender vegetables making the meal complete.

SERVES: 6 **PREP TIME:** 15 minutes **COOK TIME:** 8 hours on low
TOTAL TIME: 8 hours, 15 minutes

INGREDIENTS:

- 3 Tbsp. ketchup
- 3 Tbsp. low-sodium soy sauce
- 1 Tbsp. Sriracha
- ¼ cup honey
- ¼ cup hoisin sauce
- ½ cup low-sodium chicken broth
- ¼ tsp. salt

- 2 lb. boneless beef chuck roast
- 1 Tbsp. extra virgin olive oil
- salt and pepper
- 1 medium sweet onion, sliced into 1-inch pieces
- 1 large russet potato, peeled, cut into 1-inch pieces
- 1½ cups baby carrots, cut in half

DIRECTIONS:

In a medium bowl, whisk together the ketchup, soy sauce, sriracha, honey, hoison, chicken broth, and salt. Set aside.

Rub the beef all over with the olive oil; and season generously with salt and pepper. In a large sauté pan, over medium-high heat, brown the beef for about 2 minutes per side.

Place the browned beef on top of the onion, carrots, and potato in a 6-quart slow cooker. Give the broth mixture a whirl and pour over the top; turn to coat. Give everything one more grind of salt and pepper.

Cover and cook on low for 8 hours.

Transfer beef to a cutting board and, using two forks, shred the meat.

Serve the beef and vegetables on individual plates with some of the sauce.

Unstuffed Cabbage Roll Skillet

I love cabbage rolls. But I don't love how long it takes to prepare them. This easy skillet dish is a cabbage roll deconstructed, with all the same great components and flavors, but done in half the time. I love adding sweet raisins to mine!

SERVES: 4-6 **PREP TIME:** 10 Minutes **COOK TIME:** 25 Minutes **TOTAL TIME:** 35 Minutes

INGREDIENTS:

- 2 Tbsp. extra virgin olive oil
- 1 lb. lean ground beef
- 1 small sweet onion, diced
- 3 cloves garlic, minced
- ¾ tsp. salt
- ½ tsp. paprika
- ½ cup uncooked white rice

- ½ cup golden raisins
- 1 (15-oz.) can tomato sauce
- 1½ cups low-sodium beef broth
- 1 small head of cabbage, core removed, chopped (about 6 cups)
- sour cream or Greek yogurt, for serving (optional)

DIRECTIONS:

In a large skillet, heat the oil over medium-high. Add the beef and onion; sauté until onion is soft and no pink remains in the beef, about 3 minutes. Add in the garlic and cook for 30 seconds. Drain off fat. Stir in the salt and paprika.

Add rice, raisins, tomato sauce, broth, and cabbage to the skillet. Mix to combine. Bring to a boil.

Reduce heat to a medium simmer, cover, and cook for about 22 minutes until cabbage and rice are tender.

Serve in bowls with a dollop of sour cream or Greek yogurt, if desired.

Beef and Potato Picadillo

Picadillo *is a traditional dish in many Latin American countries; it's made with ground beef, diced tomatoes, and other ingredients that vary by region. Cuban-style typically includes olives and is served with black beans and rice. I switched it up with tomato sauce, potatoes, raisins, and almonds, served in pita halves. It's also delicious used as a filling for tacos!*

SERVES: 6 **PREP TIME:** 15 Minutes **COOK TIME:** 20 Minutes **TOTAL TIME:** 35 Minutes

INGREDIENTS:

- 1 Tbsp. extra virgin olive oil
- 1 lb. lean ground beef
- 1 small sweet onion, diced
- 2 garlic cloves, minced
- salt and pepper
- 1 medium potato, peeled, diced into small cubes
- ⅓ cup raisins
- 1 cup low-sodium chicken broth

- 1 Tbsp. apple cider vinegar
- 1 can (8-oz.) tomato sauce
- 1 tsp. salt
- ½ tsp. ground cumin
- pinch of red pepper flakes
- ⅓ cup sliced almonds
- 3 whole perforated multi-grain pita pockets, split
- chopped fresh parsley, optional
- plain Greek yogurt, optional

DIRECTIONS:

In a large nonstick skillet, warm oil over medium-high. Add beef, onion, and garlic; cook until beef is brown and onion is soft, about 3 minutes. Season with a pinch of salt and pepper. Drain off fat.

Stir in the potato, raisins, broth, vinegar, tomato sauce, salt, cumin, and red pepper flakes. Bring to a medium simmer, cover, and cook for 18–20 minutes, until potatoes are tender, but not mushy, stirring occasionally in the last 5 minutes to prevent sticking. Stir in the almonds.

Fill each pita half with the beef and potato mixture. Top with a sprinkle of parsley and a dollop of yogurt, if desired.

Italian Meatball Skillet

I make up a batch of meatballs about once a month. My favorite recipe provides about 80—that's how much I cook with them! Always having them on hand in the freezer has been a lifesaver on many occasions. They're great with spaghetti, of course, but also in soups, and easy skillet dishes like this one.

SERVES: 4 **PREP TIME:** 10 Minutes **COOK TIME:** 15 Minutes **TOTAL TIME:** 25 Minutes

INGREDIENTS:

- 1 Tbsp. extra virgin olive oil
- 1 small onion, diced
- 2 small carrots, sliced thin
- 1 medium zucchini, cut in half lengthwise, sliced into half moons
- 2 cloves garlic, minced
- salt and pepper

- 1 can (15-oz.) diced tomatoes with basil, oregano, and garlic
- 1/3 cup low-sodium beef broth
- 20 homemade or store-bought Italian meatballs, thawed if frozen
- 1 cup orzo pasta

DIRECTIONS:

Set water to boil in a medium pot.

Heat oil in a large nonstick skillet over medium-high. Add in onion, carrots, and zucchini. Sauté for about 5 minutes or until vegetables are almost tender. Add garlic and cook for 30 seconds. Season with a touch of salt and pepper.

Add in the seasoned tomatoes with their liquid, beef broth, and meatballs. Simmer over medium for about 10 minutes, stirring a few times, until meatballs are heated through. Season with a couple grinds of salt and pepper.

In the meantime, add orzo to the boiling water; cook until al dente according to package directions.

Serve meatballs and vegetables over the cooked orzo with some of the pan sauce!

Cumin-Lime Grilled Sirloin with Roasted Vegetables

My husband, Paul, is a really great eater, with only a few foods that he really dislikes. And even those he'll eat if put in front of him. At heart, he's really a meat and potatoes guy. I'm always doctoring up sirloin, either for stir-fry or a salad. So when I just grill a whole steak, his face lights up like a Christmas tree. He loves this one. The simple roasted vegetables balance out the meat perfectly.

SERVES: 4 **PREP TIME:** 10 minutes + marinating **COOK TIME:** 25 minutes
TOTAL TIME: 2 hours

INGREDIENTS:

- ⅔ cup orange juice
- 3 Tbsp. lime juice
- 2 garlic cloves, minced
- 1½ tsp. cumin
- ½ tsp. kosher salt
- ½ tsp. black pepper
- 2 Tbsp. chopped fresh parsley

- 1 lb. boneless top sirloin steak, 1-inch thick
- 8 oz. carrots, peeled, cut into 3-inch long sticks
- 8 oz. green beans, trimmed
- 2 Tbsp. extra virgin olive oil
- ½ tsp. kosher salt
- ¼ tsp. pepper

DIRECTIONS:

Combine the orange juice, lime juice, garlic, cumin, salt, pepper, and parsley in a large resealable plastic bag. Add sirloin; seal bag, removing as much air as possible, turn to coat. Marinate in the refrigerator for up to 1–4 hours.

Preheat oven to 425°F. Lightly coat 2 baking sheets with nonstick spray. Toss the carrots and green beans with the olive oil, salt, and pepper. Spread them out between the baking sheets. Roast in the oven for 25 minutes, tossing once and rotating halfway through cooking time, until tender.

In the meantime, heat a grill to medium. Drain sirloin and discard marinade. Place steak on well-oiled grill grates, cover and cook to desired doneness, turning once halfway through (8–10 minutes total for medium rare.) Take off the grill and let rest for 5 minutes.

Slice sirloin across the grain and serve with the roasted vegetables, along with some of the meat juices!

SEAFOOD

Grilled Fish Tacos with Chili-Lime Slaw

Three-Cheese Shrimp Quesadillas

Shrimp Fried Rice

Salmon Foil Packets with Whipped Caper Cream

Cajun Spiced Cod with Tomato Couscous

One-Pot Buttery Pasta with
Clams, Corn, and Capers

Shrimp Satay Ramen

Grilled Fish Tacos
with Chili-Lime Slaw

I love a good fish taco. The first time I ever had one was in San Diego; my skepticism immediately disappeared after just one bite. Granted, they were deep fried, and you can't beat that! But I don't like deep frying food in my house. It's messy and the smell of oil lingers for hours.

This grilled version is definitely a contender, though! The simple spice rub pairs perfectly with mellow Tilapia fillets, and the crunchy kicked-up coleslaw, along with soft, flavorful corn tortillas, put it over the top.

MAKES: 6 small tacos **PREP TIME:** 15 minutes **COOK TIME:** 10 minutes
TOTAL TIME: 25 minutes

INGREDIENTS:

- 2 cups coleslaw
- 3 Tbsp. plain Greek yogurt
- 2 tsp. Sriracha hot sauce
- ½ Tbsp. lime juice
- pinch of salt
- 1 Tbsp. vegetable oil
- ¼ tsp. salt

- ¼ tsp. garlic powder
- ¼ tsp. paprika
- ¼ tsp. ground coriander
- 2 (6-oz.) tilapia fish filets
- 6 (5-inch) good quality corn tortillas
- ¼ cup fresh parsley leaves, chopped
- limes, quartered, for serving

DIRECTIONS:

In a medium bowl, combine the coleslaw, yogurt, Sriracha, lime juice, and pinch of salt. Set aside.

Prepare an indoor or outdoor grill for medium-high heat.

In a small bowl, combine the vegetable oil, ¼ teaspoon of salt, garlic powder, paprika, and coriander. Pat the fish dry and rub both sides with the spice mixture. Thoroughly coat the grill grates with nonstick spray or oil. Place fish on the grill and cook for 3–4 minutes per side, depending how thick each filet is, until the fish is cooked and the flesh flakes with a fork.

About a minute before the fish is done, place tortillas on the grill to lightly toast (about 10 seconds per side—keep an eye on them so they don't burn).

Assemble the tacos by breaking up the fish into large pieces and dividing them, along with the slaw, among the tortillas. Sprinkle some parsley on top of each and an extra spritz of lime.

Serve immediately.

NOTES: *The general rule of thumb when grilling fish is 8 minutes per inch of thickness. Use this as a guide when cooking the fillets.*

Three-Cheese Shrimp Quesadillas

Basic quesadillas are taken up several notches with a combination of three different melted cheeses and seasoned shrimp. Serve with salsa verde, sour cream, and tortilla chips and guacamole!

SERVES: 4 **PREP TIME:** 15 Minutes **COOK TIME:** 15 Minutes **TOTAL TIME:** 30 Minutes

INGREDIENTS:

- 1 cup shredded Monterey Jack cheese
- 1 cup shredded Mozzarella cheese
- 1 cup shredded Cheddar cheese
- 4 scallions, diced
- 1 Tbsp. extra virgin olive oil
- 8 oz. medium shrimp, peeled and deveined
- ½ tsp. chili powder

- ¼ tsp. cumin
- salt and pepper
- 2 garlic cloves, minced
- 1 Tbsp. lime juice
- 6 tsp. unsalted butter
- 6 (8-inch) flour tortillas
- Salsa verde and/or sour cream for serving

DIRECTIONS:

In a large bowl, combine the three cheeses and scallions. Set aside.

In a large nonstick skillet, warm the olive oil over medium-high heat. Add in the shrimp, chili powder, cumin, and a pinch of salt and pepper. Cook, stirring, until shrimp are curled and are almost firm to the touch, about 2 minutes. Toss in the garlic and stir for 15 seconds, until fragrant. Drizzle in the lime juice and stir. Transfer to a cutting board and, once cool to the touch, coarsely chop.

Add shrimp to the bowl with the cheeses and toss to combine.

To assemble, spread 1 teaspoon of butter on one side of each flour tortilla. On the non-buttered side, evenly divide the shrimp mixture (about 1 cup per quesadilla.) Place another tortilla on top, buttered side up.

Clean the nonstick skillet you used for the shrimp; place over medium heat. Once the skillet is hot, cook each quesadilla for 2–3 minutes until cheese begins to melt and underside is golden. Carefully flip and cook for another 1–2 minutes until cheese is completely melted and the other tortilla is golden, as well.

Cut each quesadilla into six wedges. Serve with salsa verde and/or sour cream.

Shrimp Fried Rice

While in college, I lived off of Ramen noodles, baked potatoes, and fried rice. Who didn't, right? Fried rice is truly the ideal one-pot meal for anyone on a budget. It's super inexpensive to make, you've got your protein and vegetables all in one, it's cooked in a matter of minutes, and is quite filling. If shrimp is not your thing, try substituting it with pork or chicken.

SERVES: 4 **PREP TIME:** 15 Minutes **COOK TIME:** 7 Minutes **TOTAL TIME:** 22 Minutes

INGREDIENTS:

- 1 Tbsp. vegetable oil
- 2 Tbsp. sesame oil, divided
- ¾ lb. shrimp, peeled and deveined, diced small
- salt and pepper
- 1¼ cup frozen peas and carrots, defrosted
- 3 scallions, diced
- 2 cloves garlic, minced
- 2 large eggs, beaten
- 4 cups cold, day-old cooked long-grain white rice
- 3 Tbsp. low-sodium soy sauce
- 1 tsp. chili garlic sauce

DIRECTIONS:

In a large wok or non-stick skillet, heat the vegetable oil and 1 tablespoon sesame oil over medium-high. Season the shrimp with a touch of salt and pepper and add to the skillet. Cook for 1-2 minutes until pink; with a slotted spoon, transfer to a plate.

Add the remaining tablespoon sesame oil to the skillet. Toss in the peas and carrots, scallions, and garlic; sauté for 1 minute. Season with a sprinkle of salt and pepper. Push ingredients to the side and make a well in the middle; add eggs in the center and cook to scramble.

Return shrimp to skillet, along with the rice. Mix to combine and heat through.

Stir in the soy sauce and chili garlic sauce; taste and season with 1-2 more grinds of a salt and pepper, if necessary.

Serve in bowls and pass extra soy sauce at the table, if desired.

NOTES: *One of the keys to great fried rice is using day-old rice. Freshly cooked rice will result in soggy grains, while day-old rice helps to dry the grains out enough for a great chewy texture.*

Salmon Foil Packets with Whipped Caper Cream

I know it's hard for some people to get excited about fish in the same way, say, you would with bacon or a hot fudge sundae. But this recipe is where fish is at! It's a great take on traditional lox and cream cheese, but instead of sliced smoked salmon, whole fillets are steamed in foil packets with pickled capers, onion, and tart orange juice, then served with a fantastic creamy and salty whipped topping.

SERVES: 4 **PREP TIME:** 15 Minutes **COOK TIME:** 25 Minutes **TOTAL TIME:** 40 Minutes

INGREDIENTS:

- 4 thin slices red onion
- 4 tsp. capers, drained
- 2½ Tbsp. extra virgin olive oil, divided
- 4 (5-oz.) skinless salmon fillets
- salt and pepper
- 4 tsp. orange juice, divided

For the Caper Cream

- ½ cup cold heavy whipping cream
- 2 Tbsp. plain Greek yogurt
- 2 Tbsp. orange juice
- ⅛ tsp. salt
- ¼ tsp. Sriracha hot sauce
- ¼ cup minced red onion
- 1½ Tbsp. capers, drained and chopped

DIRECTIONS:

Preheat oven to 400°F.

Cut four sheets of aluminum foil about 14-inches long. Place 1 slice of onion and 1 teaspoon of capers in the center of each length of foil; drizzle with 1 teaspoon of the olive oil. Place salmon on the top and drizzle with 1 teaspoon of oil and 1–2 grinds of salt and pepper, and 1 teaspoon of orange juice.

Wrap sides of foil inward over the salmon and fold in top and bottom of foil to completely enclose. Place pouches on a baking sheet in a single layer. Bake until salmon is just cooked through and easily flakes with a fork, about 25 minutes.

While the fish is baking, make the caper cream. In a medium bowl, add the cream, yogurt, orange juice, salt, and Sriracha; beat with a handheld mixer until soft peaks form, about 1 minute. Fold in the minced red onion and capers. Taste and adjust salt and Sriracha, if desired.

Using a large metal spatula, transfer foil packets to plates and serve with the caper cream.

Cajun Spiced Cod
with Tomato Couscous

Take boring fish up a few notches by adding spicy Cajun seasoning and serving it with flavored couscous. The method couldn't be easier; simply bake the cod right on top of the couscous and you have a complete delicious meal and only one pan to clean up!

SERVES: 4 **PREP TIME:** 15 Minutes **COOK TIME:** 20 Minutes **TOTAL TIME:** 35 Minutes

INGREDIENTS:

- 4 (5-oz.) skinless cod fillets
- 1½ tsp. Cajun seasoning
- salt and pepper
- 2 tsp. extra virgin olive oil, divided
- 3 Tbsp. unsalted butter
- 3 scallions, diced, white and green parts divided
- 3 garlic cloves, minced
- 1¼ cups vegetable broth

- 1 can (15-oz.) diced tomatoes, undrained
- ⅓ cup frozen peas, thawed
- ½ tsp. kosher salt
- ¼ tsp. black pepper
- 1 cup plain couscous
- ½ cup fresh chopped parsley
- 1 Tbsp. lemon juice

DIRECTIONS:

Preheat oven to 450°F.

Rub the cod fillets all over with the cajun spice and season with salt and pepper to taste. Drizzle a ½ teaspoon of the olive oil over the top of each one. Set aside.

In a large nonstick ovenproof skillet, melt butter over medium-high heat. Add scallion whites and garlic; cook, stirring constantly, until scallions are softened, about 1 minute. Add the vegetable broth, tomatoes with their liquid, peas, ½ teaspoon kosher salt, and ¼ teaspoon pepper. Bring to a boil; stir in couscous and place cod fillets on top. Cover and place in the oven; bake until fish is opaque throughout and easily flakes with a fork, 20 minutes.

Remove from the oven. Careful, handle will be hot! Gently transfer fish to individual plates.

Fluff couscous with a fork; fold in the scallion greens, parsley, and lemon juice. Serve immediately with the fish.

One-Pot Buttery Pasta with Clams, Corn, and Capers

Made all in one pot, this brilliant pasta soaks up flavor from wine and chicken broth, instead of water, creating its own sauce. If you're a fan of linguine with clam sauce, you will love this!

SERVES: 4 **PREP TIME:** 15 Minutes **COOK TIME:** 10 Minutes **TOTAL TIME:** 25 Minutes

INGREDIENTS:

- 2 Tbsp. extra virgin olive oil
- 1 medium sweet onion, diced
- 4 garlic cloves, minced
- ⅓ cup white wine
- 4½ cups low-sodium chicken broth
- 12 oz. thin spaghetti
- 1 can (10-oz.) whole baby clams, drained
- ½ cup canned corn kernels, drained
- 2 Tbsp. capers, rinsed
- 2 Tbsp. lemon juice
- 2 Tbsp. unsalted butter
- ¼ tsp. red pepper flakes
- freshly ground black pepper
- ¼ cup fresh chopped parsley

DIRECTIONS:

Heat oil over medium-high in a Dutch oven pot.

Add onion to the pot and cook until softened, stirring frequently, about 3 minutes. Add garlic and cook for 15–30 seconds. Raise heat to high; add in white wine and allow liquid to reduce by half. Pour in broth; bring to a boil.

Stir in the pasta, cover, and cook for about 7 minutes until the pasta is tender and most of the liquid has absorbed.

Mix in clams, corn, capers, lemon juice, and butter. Season with the red pepper flakes and black pepper. Warm through. Toss in the parsley.

Serve immediately in individual bowls.

NOTES: *This recipe calls for **thin** spaghetti, which is in between regular and angel hair. Make sure that's what you use, or the cooking time and amount of broth will need to be adjusted.*

Shrimp Satay Ramen

You don't realize how much of a certain ingredient is in packaged food . . . until you can no longer have it! We've been saddled with peanut allergies, which has forced me to not only read labels more, but also get creative in cooking.

Luckily, my kids are not allergic to other nuts, so I just tweak everything with almond or sunflower butter. This simple Thai-inspired noodle dish uses the latter, and it's delicious!

SERVES: 4 **PREP TIME:** 15 Minutes **COOK TIME:** 10 Minutes **TOTAL TIME:** 25 Minutes

INGREDIENTS:

- 3 Tbsp. sesame oil, divided
- ¼ cup low-sodium soy sauce
- 2 Tbsp. creamy sunflower butter
- 1 Tbsp. rice vinegar
- 1 Tbsp. vegetable oil
- 1 tsp. Sriracha hot sauce
- salt and pepper

- 4 pkgs. (3-oz. each) ramen noodles, seasoning packet discarded
- 3 cloves garlic, minced
- 2 tsp. grated peeled ginger
- 1 lb. raw medium shrimp, peeled and deveined
- ½ cup frozen baby peas, defrosted
- ⅓ cup chopped fresh parsley

DIRECTIONS:

In a small bowl, whisk together 2 tablespoons of the sesame oil, soy sauce, sunflower butter, rice vinegar, vegetable oil, Sriracha, and a pinch of salt and pepper. Set aside.

Bring a large pot of water to boil. Cook ramen for 3 minutes, separating the noodles. Drain and set noodles aside.

In the same pot, heat the remaining 1 tablespoon sesame oil over medium-high. Sauté garlic and ginger for 15 seconds, stirring constantly. Add in shrimp; cook 2–3 minutes until pink and cooked through. Season with a little salt and pepper.

Add noodles back to pot, along with the peas, parsley, and soy sauce mixture. Gently toss to coat.

Serve immediately.

MEATLESS

Easy Chickpea Curry

Baked Breakfast Taquitos

Sesame Noodles with Roasted Broccoli

Egg Salad Pita Pockets

Roasted Tofu with Eggplant and Cherry Tomatoes

Huevos Rancheros Tacos

Italian Stuffed Zucchini

Eggs in Purgatory

Farfalle with Tomatoes and Beans

Tex-Mex Migas Waffles

Easy Chickpea Curry

Once upon a time I gave up eating meat, and this was one of the first introductions I had to Vegetarian cuisine that confirmed I wouldn't miss it. It's an incredibly hearty and flavorful pantry meal that can be made for just a few dollars. Even though I've long gone back to cooking with beef, pork, and chicken, this remains one of my all-time favorite recipes!

SERVES: 6 **PREP TIME:** 15 Minutes **COOK TIME:** 15 Minutes **TOTAL TIME:** 30 Minutes

INGREDIENTS:

- 3 Tbsp. extra virgin olive oil
- 1 medium sweet onion, diced small
- 3 cloves garlic, minced
- 1 Tbsp. minced fresh ginger
- 2 tsp. granulated sugar
- 2 tsp. curry powder
- 2 Tbsp. tomato paste
- ½ cup vegetable broth
- 1 can (15-oz.) chickpeas (garbanzo beans), rinsed and drained

- 1 can (15-oz.) diced tomatoes, undrained
- 1 Tbsp. lemon juice
- 2 Tbsp. unsalted butter
- 1 tsp. salt
- black pepper to taste
- 4 cups fresh baby spinach
- cooked white rice

DIRECTIONS:

In a large nonstick skillet, heat oil over medium-high. Add onion and cook, stirring frequently until softened, about 3 minutes. Add in the garlic, ginger, sugar, curry powder, and tomato paste; cook for another 1–2 minutes until thoroughly combined and fragrant.

Add vegetable broth, chickpeas, diced tomatoes with their liquid, lemon juice, and butter; season with the salt and pepper. Simmer, stirring occasionally, for another 10 minutes or so, until chickpeas are soft, but not mushy.

Stir in the spinach and cook for another minute, or until spinach wilts. Taste, and season with a little more salt and pepper if desired.

Serve over hot rice.

Baked Breakfast Taquitos

These taquitos are filled with eggs, ham, and cheese. Moist on the inside, with a crunchy exterior. Make them ahead, freeze, and have them ready in just minutes—great for grab and go mornings, and of course, dinner!

MAKES: 12 **PREP TIME:** 20 Minutes **COOK TIME:** 15 Minutes **TOTAL TIME:** 35 Minutes

INGREDIENTS:

- 1 Tbsp. unsalted butter
- 2 cups deli ham, chopped
- 6 large eggs, beaten
- 3 Tbsp. half-and-half
- salt and pepper
- 4 scallions, diced

- 12 (6-inch) flour tortillas
- 1½ cups shredded Colby Jack cheese
- cooking spray
- kosher salt
- salsa and sour cream for serving, optional

DIRECTIONS:

Preheat oven to 425°F. Line a baking sheet with foil, coated with nonstick cooking spray.

Heat the butter in a large nonstick fry pan over medium-high. Add ham and sauté until starting to crisp, 3-4 minutes. Add eggs and half-and-half to the pan and stir to scramble. Season with a touch of salt and pepper to taste. Transfer to a medium bowl. Gently mix in the scallions.

Microwave the tortillas for 20-30 seconds until pliable. Place about ¼ cup of the egg filling onto the lower third of each tortilla, followed by 2 tablespoons of the cheese. Roll up tightly and place seam-side down on the baking sheet, making sure the rolls are not touching each other. Spray the tops lightly with a little cooking spray, followed by a sprinkle of kosher salt.

Bake for 12-14 minutes until golden and crispy. Serve with salsa and/or sour cream on the side, if desired.

NOTES: *For added spice, swap out the Colby Jack cheese for Pepperjack.*

Sesame Noodles with Roasted Broccoli

I've never been addicted to anything, but I do have a rather strong relationship with sesame oil, and I can eat an entire head of roasted broccoli without coming up for air. So, it only stands to reason that I love this dish so much. The sweet and spicy sauce that coats the noodles seals the deal.

SERVES: 4 **PREP TIME:** 10 Minutes **COOK TIME:** 20 Minutes **TOTAL TIME:** 30 Minutes

INGREDIENTS:

- 1 large head broccoli, cut into florets
- 3 Tbsp. extra virgin olive oil
- salt and pepper
- 12 oz. spaghetti
- ¼ cup low-sodium soy sauce
- 2 Tbsp. rice wine vinegar
- 3 Tbsp. sesame oil

- 2 Tbsp. vegetable oil
- ½ tsp. chili garlic sauce
- 2 Tbsp. granulated sugar
- 3 cloves garlic, minced
- 2 scallion stalks, diced
- ½ Tbsp. sesame seeds

DIRECTIONS:

Preheat oven to 425°F. And bring a large pot of water to boil.

Spread broccoli on a rimmed baking sheet. Drizzle the olive oil over the florets, along with several grinds of salt and pepper; toss to coat. Place in the oven and roast for 10 minutes. Toss, and roast 10 more minutes.

Simultaneously, cook the pasta to al dente according to package instructions, about 9 minutes.

While pasta is cooking, in a medium bowl, whisk together the soy sauce, vinegar, sesame oil, vegetable oil, chili garlic sauce, sugar, garlic, and scallions.

Drain the pasta and return to the pot. Pour in sauce and toss to combine. Gently mix in the roasted broccoli.

Serve immediately with a sprinkle of sesame seeds.

Egg Salad Pita Pockets

This egg salad is simple, creamy, and delicious. It's slightly sweet, slightly tangy, and with a little crunch from dill pickles. Served up in pita pockets, it's great for a light summer meal out on the patio.

SERVES: 5 **PREP TIME:** 20 Minutes **COOK TIME:** 11 Minutes **TOTAL TIME:** 31 Minutes

INGREDIENTS:

- 8 large eggs
- 1 large dill pickle, diced small
- 2 tsp. dill pickle juice
- 2 Tbsp. mayonnaise
- 3 tsp. yellow mustard
- 2 tsp. sugar
- ¼ tsp. kosher salt
- ⅛ tsp. pepper
- pinch cracked red pepper flakes, optional
- 5 lettuce leaves
- 5 half pita pockets

DIRECTIONS:

Place the eggs in a single layer at the bottom of a medium pot. Fill with water until it reaches just 1-inch above the top of the eggs. Heat the pot on high and bring the water to a rolling boil. Turn off the heat; keep the pan on the burner, cover, and let sit for 11 minutes.

Drain out the hot water and run cold water over the eggs (this will cool them quickly and prevent further cooking. Alternatively, you can move the eggs to an ice bath with a slotted spoon.)

When the eggs are cool to the touch, peel, then dice.

In a large bowl, whisk together the diced dill pickle, dill pickle juice, mayonnaise, mustard, sugar, salt, pepper, and cracked red pepper (if using), until combined. Gently fold in the chopped eggs.

Place one lettuce leaf inside of each half pita pocket, followed by a ½ cup scoop of the egg salad. Serve with chips or extra dill pickle slices on the side!

NOTES: *Week old eggs are easier to peel than fresh eggs. I also find that it's easier to peel them when they're still slightly warm. If you want to make the hard-boiled eggs ahead of time, you can store them in a tightly sealed container and place in the refrigerator up to 5 days.*

Roasted Tofu with Eggplant and Cherry Tomatoes

I think one of the reasons that tofu gets a bad rap is because most people have never had it prepared for them in an appealing way. It's like a sponge, and needs to absorb other flavors— that's why it's so delicious in miso soup! It's also wonderful baked. With a little dusting of cornstarch, it gets crispy on the outside, but still soft on the inside. Tofu is fantastic in this quick marinade, roasted with eggplant and sweet tomatoes.

SERVES: 4 **PREP TIME:** 15 Minutes **COOK TIME:** 30 Minutes **TOTAL TIME:** 45 Minutes

INGREDIENTS:

- 1 package (14 oz) extra firm tofu
- 1 Tbsp. low-sodium soy sauce
- 1 Tbsp. rice wine vinegar
- 1 Tbsp. sesame oil
- 1 Tbsp. cornstarch

- 1 large eggplant globe, stem removed, cut into 1-inch cubes
- 4 Tbsp. extra virgin olive oil, divided
- salt and pepper
- 1 pint cherry tomatoes
- 2 tablespoons chopped fresh parsley

DIRECTIONS:

Preheat oven to 400°F. Lightly coat one large baking sheet with nonstick spray, and line another one with parchment paper.

While oven is heating up, remove tofu from packaging, pat dry with paper towels, and set on a plate lined with a paper towel. Place a small plate on top of the tofu, followed by a heavy can to weight it down and release excess liquid.

In a medium bowl, whisk together the soy sauce, vinegar, and sesame oil. Cut the tofu into ½-¾ inch cubes and gently toss in the marinade to coat. With a slotted spoon, transfer to the parchment lined baking sheet and sprinkle with the cornstarch; gently toss. Make sure pieces are not touching each other.

Spread eggplant cubes on the baking sheet coated with cooking spray and toss with 3 tablespoons of oil, and some salt and pepper to taste, until all the cubes are coated.

Place both the eggplant and the tofu in the oven for 15 minutes; stir with a spatula. Push the eggplant to one side of the baking sheet. Toss cherry tomatoes with the remaining tablespoon of oil and a sprinkle of salt and pepper and add to the baking sheet with the eggplant.

Return both baking sheets back to the oven for another 15 minutes.

Transfer roasted tofu, eggplant, and tomatoes onto a serving tray; gently toss with the parsley. Serve immediately and enjoy!

NOTES: *If you have time and remember to do so, marinate the tofu overnight, which will really deepen the flavors.*

Huevos Rancheros Tacos

Huevos rancheros is a popular breakfast enjoyed on rural Mexican farms. Traditionally, they consist of sunny-side up eggs served on fried corn tortillas, along with salsa and refried beans. These are a quick fix, eliminating the need for oil, and using scrambled eggs, which tend to have a broader appeal. Hearty, healthy, vegetarian, and absolutely delicious.

SERVES: 2 **PREP TIME:** 15 Minutes **COOK TIME:** 5 Minutes **TOTAL TIME:** 20 Minutes

INGREDIENTS:

- ⅓ cup canned pinto beans, rinsed and drained
- 1½ tsp. extra virgin olive oil
- ½ tsp. dried Italian herbs
- dash of cayenne pepper
- pinch of salt
- ½ Tbsp. unsalted butter

- 3 large eggs, beaten
- 4 (5-inch) good quality corn tortillas, warmed
- ¼ cup shredded colby jack cheese
- ¼ cup salsa
- chopped fresh cilantro, optional

DIRECTIONS:

In a small bowl mix the beans, olive oil, Italian herbs, cayenne pepper and salt to taste. Place in the microwave for 20–30 seconds until warmed through; stir, set aside, cover and keep warm.

In a large nonstick skillet, melt the butter over medium-high heat. Pour in eggs. Cook without stirring until eggs begin to set slightly on the bottom and around the edges, then stir to scramble and combine until cooked through but still glossy and moist.

Evenly distribute the scrambled eggs among the tortillas. Top with a tablespoon of cheese, a tablespoon of salsa, and some of the beans. Fold in half and allow cheese to melt. Sprinkle with some fresh chopped cilantro, if desired.

Serve immediately and enjoy!

NOTES: *If you're serving 4 people, simply double all the ingredients.*

Italian Stuffed Zucchini

There's something so fun about prepared food where the "container" can be eaten, too; soup in bread bowls and lettuce cups immediately come to mind, as do stuffed peppers and zucchini.

Here, scooped-out zucchini halves are filled with a mixture of couscous, sun-dried tomatoes, pine nuts, and spinach, then topped with Parmesan. They're quite wonderful and substantial.

SERVES: 6 **PREP TIME:** 20 Minutes **COOK TIME:** 20 Minutes **TOTAL TIME:** 40 Minutes

INGREDIENTS:

- 1½ cups vegetable broth
- 1 cup plain couscous
- 2 Tbsp. unsalted butter
- ½ tsp. salt
- 2 cloves garlic, finely minced
- 3 Tbsp. toasted pine nuts
- ⅔ cup freshly grated Parmesan cheese, divided
- ⅓ cup sun-dried tomatoes julienne cut packed in oil, drained and coarsely chopped
- 1 cup packed baby spinach, chopped
- 6 large zucchini, cut in half lengthwise, seeds scraped out
- salt and pepper

DIRECTIONS:

Preheat oven to 400°F. Prep a large baking sheet with parchment paper.

In a medium saucepan, bring vegetable broth to a boil. Remove from heat and stir in the couscous. Cover and let stand for 5 minutes, then fluff with a fork. Add butter and gently toss to melt. Add in the salt, garlic, pine nuts, ⅓ cup of the Parmesan, tomatoes, and spinach; gently stir to combine and allow spinach to wilt.

Place zucchini halves on the baking sheet, cut side up; season with a touch of salt and pepper. Fill zucchini shells with the couscous mixture. Sprinkle with the remaining Parmesan. Bake for about 20 minutes, until tender.

Serve immediately and enjoy!

NOTES: *Baby arugula can be substituted for the spinach. Chicken broth can be substituted for the vegetable broth, if you're not adhering to a vegetarian diet.*

Eggs in Purgatory

The origin of Eggs in Purgatory is apparently up for debate. Some think it's based on a dish called shakshouka, from North Africa, while others associate it with Catholicism, where the poached eggs represent souls and the fiery tomato sauce that surrounds them represent the cross between Heaven and Hell. That's way too heavy for me. Either way, it's a classic dish, and in my humble opinion, reminiscent of delicious Huevos Rancheros.

SERVES: 4 **PREP TIME:** 10 Minutes **COOK TIME:** 15 Minutes **TOTAL TIME:** 25 Minutes

INGREDIENTS:

- 1½ Tbsp. extra virgin olive oil
- ⅓ cup diced onion
- 2 garlic cloves, minced
- 1 can (15-oz.) tomato puree
- 1 tsp. dried oregano
- ¼ tsp. cumin
- ¼ tsp. paprika
- ⅛ tsp. cracked red pepper flakes
- salt and pepper
- 4 large eggs
- toasted bread for serving
- chopped fresh parsley, for serving
- freshly grated Parmesan cheese, for serving

DIRECTIONS:

Heat olive oil in a 10-inch skillet over medium. Add onion and cook, stirring until softened and translucent, about 4 minutes. Add in garlic and cook for 30 seconds until fragrant.

Reduce heat to medium-low; add in the tomato puree, oregano, cumin, paprika, cracked red pepper, and a couple grinds of salt and black pepper; simmer for 5 minutes until thickened, stirring every minute to prevent burning.

Gently crack the eggs into the sauce; cover, and let cook until the whites are set and yolk is still runny, about 5 minutes. Remove skillet from heat, uncover, and let sit for 1–2 minutes.

Serve each egg on a slice of toast; spoon over some of the sauce and garnish with chopped fresh parsley and a sprinkle of Parmesan cheese.

NOTES: *If you make your own marinara sauce and have any leftover, it would be a great substitute for the canned tomato puree.*

Farfalle with Tomatoes and Beans

This simple pasta dish is one of the reasons to keep canned tomatoes and beans stocked in your pantry. The beans supply the protein and are a great compliment to the sweet tomatoes and creamy sauce.

SERVES: 4 **PREP TIME:** 10 Minutes **COOK TIME:** 15 Minutes **TOTAL TIME:** 25 Minutes

INGREDIENTS:

- 1 lb. farfalle pasta
- 1 Tbsp. extra virgin olive oil
- 1 Tbsp. unsalted butter
- 1 medium onion, diced
- 4 cloves garlic, minced
- 1 (14-oz.) can Cannellini beans, rinsed and drained
- 1 (15-oz.) can diced tomatoes, undrained
- 1/3 cup vegetable broth
- salt and pepper
- 1/4 tsp. cracked red pepper
- 1/4 tsp. nutmeg
- 1/3 cup heavy cream
- 1/2 cup grated Parmesan cheese
- 1/3 cup chopped fresh parsley

DIRECTIONS:

Set a large pot of water to boil. Cook pasta until al dente, according to package instructions.

While the pasta is cooking, melt olive oil and butter in a large nonstick pan over medium-high heat. Add onion and sauté for 2–3 minutes until onion is soft and translucent. Add in garlic and stir for 30 seconds until fragrant.

Add beans, tomatoes with their liquid, and vegetable broth; gently stir to combine. Let simmer for 10 minutes. Season with the salt, pepper, cracked red pepper, and nutmeg. Reduce heat to low and add the cream. Stir in the Parmesan and parsley.

Add the cooked pasta to the sauce and mix thoroughly. Adjust seasoning, if necessary. Serve hot and enjoy!

Tex-Mex Migas Waffles

Growing up in California, I never got to experience a Waffle House, since most of them are located in the South. So, when I was traveling through Atlanta, Georgia several years ago, it was one of the first stops I made. And then I went back every morning until my trip was over.

While nothing beats a traditional waffle with butter and syrup, I've played with many variations. This one incorporates some of my favorite Mexican flavors and is perfect for dinner, served with some Spanish rice and refried beans.

SERVES: 4 **PREP TIME:** 15 Minutes **COOK TIME:** 6 Minutes **TOTAL TIME:** 21 Minutes

INGREDIENTS:

- 8 large eggs
- 4 small good quality corn tortillas, cut into small pieces
- ¾ cup diced red bell pepper
- 1 cup finely diced sweet onion
- 1 clove garlic, minced
- 1 cup shredded Pepper Jack cheese
- 2 scallions, diced
- ½ tsp. salt
- ½ tsp. pepper
- chopped fresh cilantro, for serving
- salsa, for serving
- sour cream, for serving

DIRECTIONS:

Preheat a waffle iron to medium.

In a large bowl, whisk the eggs. Add the tortillas, bell pepper, onion, garlic, cheese, scallion, salt, and pepper. Mix to combine.

Coat both top and bottom waffle iron grids with nonstick cooking spray. Pour some of the egg mixture onto each section of the waffle iron, making sure all those goodies that fall to the bottom of the bowl get included. Close the lid and cook until the eggs are no longer runny, about 2–3 minutes.

Using an offset spatula, loosen the migas from the grids and transfer to individual plates.

Repeat with the remaining mixture.

Serve immediately with a sprinkle of chopped cilantro and some salsa or sour cream.

NOTES: *Spicy Pepper Jack cheese can be replaced with Monterey Jack or Cheddar.*

SOUP

Broccoli Bisque

Sweet and Sour Noodle Bowl

Meatball Soup with Pearl Couscous

Tortellini Minestrone

Cauliflower Cheddar Soup

Kitchen Sink Italian Soup

Egg Drop Soup

Broccoli Bisque

This creamy soup is tangy, rich, and simply sublime—comfort food on a cold day and one of the best ways to eat broccoli. It's simple enough for a busy weeknight, but elegant enough for a fancy dinner party.

MAKES: 6 Cups **PREP TIME:** 15 Minutes **COOK TIME:** 10 Minutes
TOTAL TIME: 25 Minutes

INGREDIENTS:

- 2 lbs. broccoli, stalk removed, and cut into florets
- 1 medium sweet onion, diced
- 4 cups vegetable broth, divided
- 2 Tbsp. unsalted butter
- ¼ cup flour
- 2 tsp. salt
- ⅛ tsp. ground black pepper
- 1 cup heavy cream
- 1 cup plain Greek yogurt
- ½ Tbsp. lemon juice

DIRECTIONS:

Place broccoli and onion in a medium pot with 1½ cups of the broth. Bring the broth to a boil, reduce heat to medium-high, cover, and let simmer until the vegetables are tender, about 6 minutes.

Place mixture in a blender and puree until smooth; set aside.

In the same pot that was used for simmering the broccoli, melt the butter. Add flour, salt, and pepper; stir frequently for 1-2 minutes. Do not allow the flour to burn.

Stir in remaining 2½ cups broth and increase the heat. Continue stirring until the mixture comes to a boil. Add the vegetable puree and heavy cream into the pot. Whisk yogurt into the mixture, followed by lemon juice.

Stir until heated through, then ladle into bowls.

Sweet and Sour Noodle Bowl

This dish is proof that you can take a 20 cent package of noodles and make it taste like you spent 15 dollars on it. With a few pantry items and fresh vegetables, this light and bright soup will leave your lips tingling!

SERVES: 4 **PREP TIME:** 15 Minutes **COOK TIME:** 10 Minutes **TOTAL TIME:** 25 Minutes

INGREDIENTS:

- 4 pkgs. (3-oz. each) ramen noodles, broken in half, flavor packet discarded
- 7 cups low-sodium chicken broth
- ¾ cup rice wine vinegar
- 2 Tbsp. Sriracha hot sauce
- ¼ cup granulated sugar
- 1½ tsp. ginger paste or 1 tsp. freshly grated ginger

- 3 scallions, diced
- ¼ cup diced radishes
- ¼ cup diced cucumber
- ¼ cup shredded carrot
- ¼ cup freshly chopped parsley

DIRECTIONS:

Bring water to boil in a large pot. Cook noodles according to package directions, about 3 minutes; drain. Set aside.

In the same pot, add chicken broth, vinegar, Sriracha, sugar, and ginger. Bring to a simmer then remove from heat. Add noodles back into the pot, along with the scallions.

Spoon into shallow bowls and top mixture with radishes, cucumber, carrot, and parsley.

NOTES: *Live with a bunch of meat eaters? Heat a bit of olive oil in the pot after draining the noodles, season some diced up pork with salt and pepper and cook for a couple of minutes. Transfer to a bowl and proceed with the recipe. Add back in at the end.*

Meatball Soup with Pearl Couscous

Reminiscent of Italian Wedding soup, this is sans cheese and egg, but with added pearl couscous. The broth is very easy and quite light. Hearty, delicious, warm-your-soul soup that's perfect for a cold dreary day. Keep premade or store bought frozen meatballs on hand and it comes together really fast!

SERVES: 4 **PREP TIME:** 10 Minutes **COOK TIME:** 15 Minutes **TOTAL TIME:** 25 Minutes

INGREDIENTS:

- 2 Tbsp. extra virgin olive oil
- 1 large sweet onion, finely diced
- salt and pepper
- ¼ tsp. cracked red pepper flakes
- ¼ tsp. dried oregano
- 1 carton (48-oz.) low-sodium chicken broth (about 6½ cups)
- 1 Tbsp. apple cider vinegar
- 24 homemade or store-bought small cooked seasoned meatballs, thawed if frozen
- ½ cup pearl couscous
- 3 cups fresh baby spinach

DIRECTIONS:

In a large Dutch oven or heavy pot, warm the olive oil over medium-high heat. Add the onions and sauté, stirring, until softened and translucent, about 3 minutes. Season with a bit of salt and pepper, the red pepper flakes, and oregano.

Pour in the chicken broth and vinegar; bring to a boil.

Add in the meatballs and couscous; reduce heat and simmer for 10 minutes. Take off heat and add in the spinach; stir until wilted.

Serve in bowls with some crusty bread on the side!

Tortellini Minestrone

I can't believe there was once a time I didn't care for soup. Now I love it! Brothy, creamy, thick, loaded with vegetables, or not—all kinds! This one is great because it utilizes basic pantry staples with added cheese filled pasta and baby arugula. Ready in under a half hour.

SERVES: 4 **PREP TIME:** 10 Minutes **COOK TIME:** 15 Minutes **TOTAL TIME:** 25 Minutes

INGREDIENTS:

- 3 Tbsp. extra virgin olive oil
- 1 medium sweet onion, diced
- 2 medium carrots, sliced thin
- 2 cloves garlic, minced
- ½ tsp. kosher salt, divided
- ⅛ tsp. black pepper
- ⅛ tsp. cracked red pepper flakes

- 6 cups low-sodium chicken broth
- 1 can (15-oz.) diced tomatoes with basil, garlic, and oregano, undrained
- ¼ cup finely grated Parmesan cheese
- 1 pkg. (9-oz.) refrigerated 3-cheese tortellini pasta
- 1½ cups baby arugula

DIRECTIONS:

Heat the olive oil in a large pot over medium-high. Add onion, carrots, garlic, ¼ teaspoon of the salt, black pepper, and red pepper flakes. Sauté, stirring frequently, until the vegetables are softened, about 7 minutes.

Pour in the chicken broth, along with the diced tomatoes, and the remaining ¼ teaspoon of salt. Bring to a boil; add tortellini, then reduce heat to a medium simmer. Cook for 8-9 minutes until pasta is tender. Stir in Parmesan and arugula and allow greens to wilt.

Ladle into bowls and sprinkle a little extra Parmesan on top, if desired.

Cauliflower Cheddar Soup

You won't miss the cream is this Cheddar Soup! Cauliflower, potatoes, and cheddar cheese are the stars here, and they are sure to comfort you on the coldest of nights.

MAKES: 8 Cups **PREP TIME:** 15 Minutes **COOK TIME:** 20 Minutes
TOTAL TIME: 35 Minutes

INGREDIENTS:

- 2 Tbsp. unsalted butter
- 1 medium sweet onion, diced
- 2 cloves garlic, minced
- Kosher salt and pepper
- cracked red pepper flakes
- 1 sprig fresh thyme
- 1 medium potato, peeled and diced into ¼-inch cubes

- 1 small head cauliflower, chopped into small florets (about 4 cups)
- 32 oz. vegetable broth
- 1 cup shredded sharp cheddar cheese, plus more for serving
- 2½ tsp. Dijon mustard

DIRECTIONS:

Melt the butter in a large pot or Dutch oven over medium-high heat. Add the onion and cook, stirring occasionally, until slightly softened, about 3 minutes. Add in the garlic and cook, stirring constantly, for 15 seconds until fragrant. Season with salt, pepper, and a pinch of cracked red pepper flakes.

Mix in the thyme, potato, cauliflower, and vegetable broth; bring to a boil. Lower the heat to a simmer, cover, and let cook for about 15 minutes until the vegetables are tender. Dig out the thyme sprig and discard. Remove from heat and stir in the cheese and mustard.

Puree with a hand-held immersion blender for a chunky texture (or a regular blender for a smoother texture, working in batches.) Taste and adjust seasoning, if necessary.

Serve warm topped with additional shredded cheese and croutons.

Kitchen Sink Italian Soup

This soup came together one night several years ago when we had reached the end of the week, but I hadn't gone grocery shopping yet. The refrigerator was bare and I was about to serve cereal for dinner. So, I grabbed what I had on hand and made soup. It remains a family favorite today. Smoked sausage is always a lifesaver!

SERVES: 6 **PREP TIME:** 15 Minutes **COOK TIME:** 20 Minutes **TOTAL TIME:** 35 Minutes

INGREDIENTS:

- 2 Tbsp. extra virgin olive oil
- 1 medium sweet onion, diced small
- 2 medium carrots, peeled, sliced thin
- 10 oz. smoked sausage or polska kielbasa, diced
- 2 garlic cloves, minced
- salt and pepper
- ½ tsp. dried Italian herbs
- ⅛ tsp. crushed red pepper flakes

- 1 can (15-oz.) diced tomatoes, undrained
- 1 carton (32-oz.) low-sodium chicken broth
- 1 can (15-oz.) white navy beans, rinsed and drained
- ⅓ cup Acini di Pepe pasta
- Fresh chopped parsley, optional
- Grated parmesan cheese, optional

DIRECTIONS:

In a large Dutch oven or pot, warm the olive oil over medium-high heat. Add in the onion, carrots, and kielbasa; sauté for 3 minutes, stirring frequently. Add in the garlic and stir for 15 seconds until fragrant. Season with a few grinds of salt and pepper, the Italian herbs, and cracked red pepper.

Add in the tomatoes with their liquid and chicken broth; bring to a boil. Stir in the beans and pasta; turn down the heat to medium and simmer for 10 minutes.

Serve warm with a sprinkle of parsley, freshly grated Parmesan, and some crusty Italian bread!

NOTES: *I like a thick chunky soup. Acini di Pepe will continue to plump up as the soup rests. If you like your soup thinner, reduce the pasta down to ¼ cup.*

Egg Drop Soup

This renowned Chinese favorite is also known as Egg Flower Soup. True to its name, beaten egg is swirled into hot broth right before serving, creating delicate noodle-like ribbons. Using the highest quality stock is critical to its flavor. While usually vegetarian, feel free to add cooked chicken, shrimp, or tofu for a heartier meal. Ready in just 15 minutes!

MAKES: 6 Cups **PREP TIME:** 10 Minutes **COOK TIME:** 5 Minutes
TOTAL TIME: 15 Minutes

INGREDIENTS:

- 3 Tbsp. cornstarch
- ¼ cup water
- 6 cups high-quality vegetable stock
- 8 whole scallion stalks, diced (about ¾ cup)
- 3 oz. crimini mushrooms, chopped
- ¼ tsp. granulated sugar

- ¼ tsp. salt
- ¼ tsp. pepper
- 3 Tbsp. low-sodium soy sauce
- 1 tsp. sesame oil
- 3 large eggs, beaten

DIRECTIONS:

In a small bowl, whisk together the cornstarch and water until thoroughly combined.

In a medium pot, whisk together the vegetable stock, scallions, mushrooms, sugar, salt, pepper, soy sauce, sesame oil, and cornstarch mixture; heat over medium-high until boiling.

Once broth reaches a boil, remove from the heat. Using a fork, stir the broth in a circular motion, while slowly pouring the eggs into the soup, creating ribbons.

Serve in individual bowls.

NOTES: Chicken stock can be substituted for the vegetable stock, but the flavor won't be as rich. Sriracha hot sauce can also be added for a kick.

SWEETS

Cranberry-Almond Chocolate Bark

Easy Creamy Coconut Pie

Cookies and Cream Cheesecake Parfaits

Strawberry Sauce

Chocolate Chip Cookie Skillet

One-Bowl Fudgy Brownies

Ricotta Blintzes

Cinnamon Roll Pastry Twists

Cranberry-Almond Chocolate Bark

Wedges of chocolate bark are super easy to make, incredibly versatile, and simply delicious. Use a combination of chocolate, nuts, and dried fruit of your choice. This blend of semi-sweet and white chocolate, studded with almonds and cranberries is one of my favorites. It makes for a great holiday gift if you can part with any of it!

MAKES: 1 pound **PREP TIME:** 10 Minutes **CHILL TIME:** 20 Minutes
TOTAL TIME: 30 Minutes

INGREDIENTS:

- 1 cup semi-sweet chocolate chips
- 1 cup white chocolate chips
- ½ cup lightly salted roasted whole almonds
- ½ cup dried cranberries

DIRECTIONS:

Line an 8 x 10 baking sheet with parchment paper.

Place semi-sweet chocolate chips in a small microwave safe bowl. Microwave for 1 minute; stir. Microwave at additional 10–20 second intervals, stirring until melted and smooth. Place white chocolate chips in a separate bowl and repeat the process.

Stir almonds and cranberries into the melted semi-sweet chocolate. Spread onto the lined baking sheet, to the edges. Drizzle the melted white chocolate over the semi-sweet mixture; cut through with a knife in a swirling motion to create a marble looking effect.

Chill in the freezer for 20 minutes or until set. Break into pieces and enjoy!

NOTES: *Refrigerate any leftovers in an airtight container.*

Easy Creamy Coconut Pie

This is one of the most popular recipes on my blog, and requested by my family constantly. Since it only takes five minutes to prepare, I can see why. Sweet, buttery, crispy, and truly wonderful, I've even witnessed coconut haters devour a slice!

SERVES: 6 **PREP TIME:** 5 Minutes **COOK TIME:** 1 hour **TOTAL TIME:** 1 hour, 5 minutes

INGREDIENTS:

- 3 eggs
- 1½ cups granulated sugar
- 1 cup unsweetened flaked coconut
- ½ cup (1 stick) unsalted butter, melted
- 1 Tbsp. white wine vinegar
- 1 tsp. vanilla extract
- pinch of salt
- 1 (9-inch) store-bought frozen or homemade pie shell

DIRECTIONS:

Preheat oven to 350°F.

In a medium bowl, mix all of the filling ingredients until well combined; pour into the pie shell.

Place pie on a cookie sheet and bake for 1 hour. Let set and cool completely before slicing.

Cookies and Cream Cheesecake Parfaits

This recipe is dedicated to my friend Melissa, who loves Oreos just as much as I do. They are my absolute favorite store-bought cookie and a serving size of two is never enough. Nothing beats dunking them in a cold glass of milk, but these easy, creamy no-bake parfaits are a close second.

SERVES: 4 **PREP TIME:** 25 Minutes **TOTAL TIME:** 25 Minutes

INGREDIENTS:

- 15 Oreo cookies
- ⅔ cup heavy cream
- ¾ cup powdered sugar, divided
- 1 pkg. (8-oz.) cream cheese
- 1 tsp. vanilla
- 2 Tbsp. milk

DIRECTIONS:

Place the Oreo cookies in a food processor and pulse several times until crumbs form. Transfer to a bowl.

In a large bowl, beat heavy cream with an electric mixer until it starts to thicken; slowly add in ¼ cup of the powdered sugar. Continue to mix until thickened and stiff peaks form. (Do not overbeat or it will become thick and clumpy.) Pour into a bowl; set aside.

In the same bowl (no need to rinse out), beat the cream cheese until smooth. Continue mixing and add in the remaining ½ cup powdered sugar, vanilla, and milk. Beat until well combined.

With a spatula, gently fold the whipped cream into the cream cheese mixture until just combined.

Alternate the cheesecake mousse with the cookie crumbs in small tumbler glasses. Continue layering depending on the size of your glasses.

Serve and enjoy!

NOTES: *To make assembly easiest, fill a large resealable plastic bag with the mousse mixture, cut off a small corner, and pipe into the glasses.*

Strawberry Sauce

Anyone who has followed my blog for a decent amount of time knows that my son, Trevor, has a thing for strawberries. He has craved them since toddlerhood. One time, my friend Heidi brought over a bushel of them and I think he had an out-of-body experience.

I make this strawberry sauce just for him and always have a jar of it in the refrigerator. It's fantastic drizzled over pound cake, angel food cake, pancakes, waffles, yogurt, or ice cream. Or, if you're like Trevor, just eat it off a spoon.

MAKES: 1½ cups **PREP TIME:** 10 Minutes **COOK TIME:** 20 Minutes
TOTAL TIME: 30 minutes + chilling

INGREDIENTS:

- 1 lb. fresh strawberries, stems removed, hulled, and diced small
- ½ cup granulated sugar
- ¼ cup water
- 1½ Tbsp. lemon juice

DIRECTIONS:

Combine all of the ingredients in a small saucepan. Cook over medium-low for about 20 minutes, stirring every once in a while to prevent burning and bubbling over.

Remove from heat and allow to cool entirely. Transfer to a mason jar or container with a tight fitting lid. Store in the refrigerator for up to 1 week.

NOTES: *If you want more of a syrupy consistency, cut the water down to 2 tablespoons. Sauce will thicken as it cools.*

Chocolate Chip Cookie Skillet

It's your favorite classic cookie, made in a skillet! No need to scoop individual balls, or rotate cookie sheets. This soft and chewy, ooey-gooey dessert will satisfy anyone's cookie craving.

SERVES: 8 **PREP TIME:** 15 Minutes **COOK TIME:** 20 Minutes **TOTAL TIME:** 35 Minutes

INGREDIENTS:

- 6 Tbsp. unsalted butter, room temperature
- ½ cup granulated sugar
- ⅓ cup packed brown sugar
- 1 large egg
- 1 tsp. vanilla extract
- 1 cup flour
- ½ tsp. baking soda
- ½ tsp. coarse salt
- ½ cup semisweet chocolate chips
- ½ cup chopped walnuts
- vanilla ice cream, optional
- chocolate syrup, optional

DIRECTIONS:

Preheat oven to 350°F. Coat a 10-inch cast iron skillet with nonstick spray; set aside.

In a large bowl, combine together the butter and both sugars with a handheld mixer until creamy.

Beat in the egg and vanilla, followed by the flour, baking soda, and salt. Stir in the chocolate chips and walnuts.

Transfer mixture to the skillet, spreading it with a spatula to fill up the pan. Bake for 20-22 minutes until golden brown and set in the center. Let cool 5 minutes before slicing.

Top with vanilla cream and/or chocolate syrup!

One-Bowl Fudgy Brownies

If a cookie, donut, piece of cake, slice of pie, or brownie were sitting in front of my daughter, Haley, she would always choose the brownie. She'd want the others, of course, but if she had to choose, the brownie would win. Every time. Fudgy, chocolaty, handheld . . . what's not to love? And since these only require one bowl and five minutes of prep, I love them, too!

SERVES: 15 **PREP TIME:** 5 Minutes **COOK TIME:** 25 Minutes **TOTAL TIME:** 30 Minutes

INGREDIENTS:

- 1¾ cups flour
- ¾ cup unsweetened cocoa powder
- 2 cups granulated sugar
- 1 tsp. salt
- 5 large eggs
- 1 cup vegetable oil
- ⅓ cup chopped walnuts
- ½ cup milk chocolate chips, divided

DIRECTIONS:

Preheat oven to 350°F. Coat a 9 x 13 pan with nonstick cooking spray; set aside.

In a large bowl, mix together the flour, cocoa powder, sugar, salt, eggs, oil, walnuts, and ¼ cup of the chocolate chips until combined.

Spread batter evenly into the prepared pan. Sprinkle remaining ¼ cup of chocolate chips over the top.

Bake for 25 minutes or until a toothpick inserted comes out almost clean.

Let cool completely before cutting.

NOTES: *Walnuts aren't your thing? Just leave them out!*

Ricotta Blintzes

Blintzes were a real treat growing up in my house, only reserved for special occasions. A paper-thin crepe is wrapped around a silky sweet cheese filling, which is then pan fried, and served with powdered sugar and jam. I'd say that qualifies as special!

The filling for blintzes ranges from farmer's cheese, to cottage cheese, to cream cheese, to mascarpone, to creme fraiche. My favorite is with a combination of whole ricotta and cream cheese.

MAKES: 10 **PREP TIME:** 15 Minutes **COOK TIME:** 20 Minutes **TOTAL TIME:** 35 Minutes

INGREDIENTS:

- 1½ cups whole ricotta cheese
- 4 oz. cream cheese, softened
- 1 egg
- 3 Tbsp. powdered sugar, plus more for serving
- 1 tsp. vanilla extract
- 10 (8-inch) fresh crepes
- 2 Tbsp. unsalted butter, divided
- jam of your choice

DIRECTIONS:

In a medium bowl, beat together the ricotta cheese, cream cheese, egg, powdered sugar, and vanilla with a handheld electric mixer until thoroughly combined.

Forming the blintzes is like a burrito. Spoon ¼ cup of the cheese filling along the lower third of each crepe, leaving a 1-inch border on the sides. Fold the bottom edge away from you to cover the filling; then fold the 2 sides into the center. Roll the crepe away from you a couple of times to completely enclose like a neat little package, ending with the seam side down.

Heat a large nonstick skillet over medium. Melt 1 tablespoon butter. Place as many blintzes as will comfortably fit in the pan without over-crowding, and fry for about 2 minutes per side until crisp and golden. Transfer blintzes to a foil-lined baking sheet. Repeat with the other blintzes, adding the remaining tablespoon of butter to the pan if necessary. Place baking sheet with all the blintzes in the oven for about 10 minutes so the cheese warms and sets.

Using a spatula, transfer the blintzes to serving plates. Spoon jam on top and dust with powdered sugar. Serve immediately.

NOTES: *If using refrigerated crepes, warm them slightly so they are pliable and don't crack while rolling. If you don't wish to serve the blintzes right away, they can be refrigerated for up to 2 days or frozen (between layers of waxed paper) for up to 2 months.*

Cinnamon Roll Pastry Twists

Love cinnamon rolls, but intimidated to work with yeast? Fear not! These twists give you the same flavor, without all the work. Puff pastry is coated with melted butter, cinnamon, and sugar, is baked, and then drizzled with a silky cream cheese glaze. So good!

MAKES: 20 **PREP TIME:** 20 Minutes **COOK TIME:** 15 Minutes **TOTAL TIME:** 35 Minutes

INGREDIENTS:

- ½ pkg. puff pastry (1 sheet)
- ½ tsp. cinnamon
- 2½ Tbsp. brown sugar
- flour for dusting
- 2 Tbsp. unsalted butter, melted

- 2 oz. cream cheese, softened
- 1 cup powdered sugar
- 2 Tbsp. milk
- 1 tsp. vanilla extract

DIRECTIONS:

Allow puff pastry to thaw per package instructions.

Preheat oven to 400°F. Line two baking sheets with parchment paper; set aside.

In a small bowl, combine the cinnamon and brown sugar.

Lightly dust work surface and a rolling pin with flour. Roll out puff pastry to a 12 x 10 rectangle. Cut crosswise into two even rectangles.

With a pastry brush, coat both pieces of the pastry with the butter. Sprinkle one rectangle with the cinnamon-sugar mixture. Place the other pastry piece on top and gently roll them together with the rolling pin.

Using a pizza cutter or sharp knife, slice into short strips, about 6 inches tall and ¼-inch wide. Pinch the ends together and twist. Place onto the lined baking sheets about 2 inches apart. Bake for approximately 15 minutes or until golden brown. Let cool.

While the twists are baking, whisk together the cream cheese, powdered sugar, milk, and vanilla in a medium bowl until thoroughly combined and a drizzling consistency is reached. (If it's too thick, add more milk. If too thin, add more powdered sugar.)

Either drizzle over the twists or place in a small bowl for dipping.

Cooking Measurement Equivalents

CUPS	TABLESPOONS	FLUID OUNCES
⅛ cup	2 Tbsp.	1 fl. oz.
¼ cup	4 Tbsp.	2 fl. oz.
⅓ cup	5 Tbsp. + 1 tsp.	
½ cup	8 Tbsp.	4 fl. oz.
⅔ cup	10 Tbsp. + 2 tsp.	
¾ cup	12 Tbsp.	6 fl. oz.
1 cup	16 Tbsp.	8 fl. oz.

CUPS	FLUID OUNCES	PINTS/QUARTS/GALLONS
1 cup	8 fl. oz.	½ pint
2 cups	16 fl. oz.	1 pint = ½ quart
3 cups	24 fl. oz.	1½ pints
4 cups	32 fl. oz.	2 pints = 1 quart
8 cups	64 fl. oz.	2 quarts = ½ gallon
16 cups	128 fl. oz.	4 quarts = 1 gallon

Other Helpful Equivalents

1 Tbsp.	3 tsp.
8 oz.	½ lb.
16 oz.	1 lb.

Metric Measurement Equivalents

Approximate Weight Equivalents

OUNCES	POUNDS	GRAMS
4 oz.	¼ lb.	113 g
5 oz.		142 g
6 oz.		170 g
8 oz.	½ lb.	227 g
9 oz.		255 g
12 oz.	¾ lb.	340 g
16 oz.	1 lb.	454 g

Approximate Volume Equivalents

CUPS	US FLUID OUNCES	MILLILITERS
⅛ cup	1 fl. oz.	30 ml
¼ cup	2 fl. oz.	59 ml
½ cup	4 fl. oz.	118 ml
¾ cup	6 fl. oz.	177 ml
1 cup	8 fl. oz.	237 ml

Other Helpful Equivalents

½ tsp.	2½ ml
1 tsp.	5 ml
1 Tbsp.	15 ml

Index

Acknowledgments

It's hard to believe that this gal, who once worked in the music industry, didn't know a thing about food, and often ate potato chips for dinner, just wrote a cookbook.

But I did. And it's awesome. For me—and hopefully for you!

Just like an actor needs a good director, and a professional athlete needs a great coach, a book needs a publisher! Thanks to Cedar Fort for making my little dream a reality.

And rarely is a personal or professional achievement reached without the help of family, friends, and colleagues.

I don't think my husband, Paul, had any idea what he was getting himself into back in 2009 when he suggested I start a food blog. We have often joked that it's like our third child. I spend endless hours caring for it, getting mad at it, worrying about it, and loving it. And I could not do it without him. He has washed more dishes for me, without complaint, than you can imagine. He is a hands-on Dad, folder of laundry, scrubber of toilets, master builder, spell-checker, human Google, and makes me laugh like no other. Love you, Pup.

To Haley and Trevor. My two little humans I never knew I wanted and now could never ever live without. The best taste-testers a mom could dream of. You're not allowed to move away, ok? Okay.

My parents Ethan and Sharon, who paved the way, are nothing but supportive, and play a mean game of cards. Every kid should be so lucky.

My sister, Jen, who shares my love for cooking. My cheerleader. My best friend.

My posse: Heather Campbell, Cher Ekasala, Meghan Gorham, Karen Hawk, Monique Judge, Heidi Petz, Christy Savage, Alicia Scull, and Brandi Solis. Thanks for doing life with me. It really does take a village.

To Kimberley Petz and KAP Photography for the use of your kitchen and wonderful author photo.

To Melissa Ortiz and Rebecca Lindamood who have been on this journey with me since the very beginning!

To Kathy Strahs, Tammy Crystal McDonald, and Crystal Moritz—mad respect for these ladies.

To the food blogging community, which is plentiful! I have witnessed generosity beyond measure and some amazing acts of kindness over the years. So many colleagues have become real life friends. Trish, Dorothy, Karen, Heather, Glory, Tanya, Lisa, Cathy, and Hayley. Love you gals!

And most important, my readers! Belly Full would be nothing without them. From the mom who started following me after I published my first blog post seven years ago, and still with me today, to the Dad who found me just last week. The comments, the shares, and the friendly e-mails are what all makes it worth it. Your support is my lifeline and I appreciate you all more than you will ever know!

About the Author

Amy Flanigan is a graphic designer, turned stay-at-home mom, turned writer and photographer for the popular family-friendly food blog, Belly Full.

What began as a hobby back in 2009, supplying food for gatherings and play dates, quickly evolved into a full-time job where she started cataloging her recipes online so that everyone could access her good eats. She realized that she and so many others were desperate for quick and easy meals to feed their families.

Her creations have been featured on Parade Magazine, HERLIFE Magazine, The Huffington Post, BuzzFeed, and all around the internet.

Amy lives in Northern California with her husband and two children and is a sucker for all animals, a good book, a funny joke, the smell of freshly baked bread, and pie. Any kind.

SCAN to visit

www.bellyfull.net